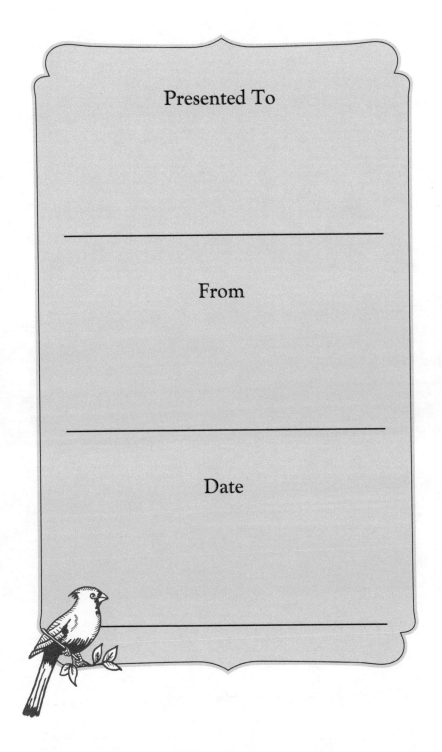

Presented To

_____

From

_____

Date

_____

Cardinal Rules
for a
Happy Home
A 90 Day Couples Devotional

Ed Young

For information contact:

The Winning Walk
6400 Woodway Drive
Houston, TX 77057
www.winningwalk.org
www.second.org

Printed in the United States of America

ISBN: 978-1-934590-83-6

Acknowledgements

Let me express appreciation to these who have helped with this project, and who know all about my Cardinal family:

My writing assistant, Angel Texada, who wordsmithed and distilled my sermons into these daily devotionals.

My office staff: Becky Ayers, Betty Brockman, Cris Parrish, Toni Richmond, and Beverly Gambrell, who bring their unique gifts and play significant roles in every book project I undertake.

Thank you, ladies, for your undying faithfulness to the Lord and your help in keeping me afloat in so many ways as we serve Him in the Second Family.

And to the Second Family, thank you for allowing me the great privilege of serving as your pastor for 34 years. I truly do believe with all my heart the best is yet to be!

Dedication

How could I write a book about a Happy Home without dedicating it to the love of my life, Jo Beth? She has helped me build a home on the solid foundation of Jesus Christ. Ours is a marriage based on a deep and abiding commitment to Christ and to each other. As a result, our Happy Home has been filled with an abundance of blessings, including ten precious grandchildren.

Jo Beth and I have hosted The Cardinals you will read about, and who inspired the title of this book, for many summers over the years. She has photographed them, fed them, and enjoyed them alongside me. I am not sure what attracts them more – the food I give them, or Jo Beth's warmth, hospitality, and gentle spirit!

Introduction

Every summer we have special houseguests. They are a beautiful couple. As I observe their interaction, I am struck by how much we can learn from them in regard to the home and to marriage. This couple just happens to be cardinals. Yes, birds. You see, in God's infinite wisdom, all of creation has meaning and purpose. So, when I see an illustration of marriage beautifully demonstrated in these scarlet-feathered guests, I pay attention. After all, the male cardinal is designed for that very purpose: to be noticed.

Our home has a sliding glass door that when opened exposes our entire living room to the outdoors. It is from this vantage point, unencumbered by the glass barrier, that I begin to encounter our guests. The male cardinal is the one I usually see first. Initially, he comes around tentatively. Sensing that there is someone or something nearby, he checks for safety. I toss a little bread his way and watch. He approaches it carefully, takes the food and flies away out of my sight.

Over time he becomes more comfortable and deems my home a safe place. It is only then that we begin to see the female. She is beautiful in her own way. More demure and modestly colored, her beak is the only part of her body that is a vivid red. In their relationship, the male always leads. If other birds, animals, or humans approach, he goes into an elaborate distraction dance. He swoops, soars, sings, and flaps. Beautiful and fascinating to watch, all eyes focus on him. But if you watch carefully, the female makes her get-away. Quietly she retreats to safety somewhere unseen.

I like this demonstration of bravado. The male takes charge, and at all costs to himself, he protects his wife. I can draw a parallel to Ephesians 5:25, *"Husbands, love your wives, just as Christ also loved the church and gave Himself up for her...."*

Another aspect I find fascinating about my friends The Cardinals is his provision for her. He feeds her. He actually catches the food, chews it in his own mouth, and then tenderly, beak-to-beak, places the nourishment into her mouth. Paul writes in I Timothy 5:8, *"But if anyone does not provide for his own, and especially for those of his household, he has denied the faith and is worse than an unbeliever."*

Before the cardinals mate – which some studies indicate they do for life – there is a courtship. The courtship involves a sort of flirtation. When the male finds a female he is interested in, he begins a time of wooing and gentle affection. This is the first time I see him provide food for her. In the courtship, the male will take one seed or one small piece of food and gently and slowly advance toward her. If she allows him to completely approach her, he gently leans in and touches his beak to hers…she opens her mouth and the male gingerly places the treat in her mouth. It looks just like a kiss. This is different from the nourishing provision we see him give her once they are a couple. Once she has accepted his overtures, the male bird sings what is known as the cardinal love song. He goes to a high place and sings his heart song at the top of his lungs. Legend has it that he is declaring his joy to all who will listen.

The female charmingly demonstrates God's design as well. She is a helpmate. She gathers and lines the nest on which both the male and the female perch. The lining of the nest is intricate, providing both comfort and safety for her family. When eggs are laid, we see the male cardinal more often as he is hunting and gathering more food to take home to her. After the fledgling birds are hatched, the male and the female take turns attending the babies. Each time the mother cardinal leaves the nest, she sings a lullaby. Experts believe this song has two purposes: one is to soothe the babies into a calm state in preparation for her absence. The second purpose is to summon the father. As soon as she flies off, he appears and covers the babies with his scarlet wings. They parent as a team.

I could go on and on about the life-lessons we can extrapolate from observing these beautiful creatures. As this couple has become more familiar with us, they have come all the way inside our home and even perched on our dining table. Such trust and familiarity has been earned over a long period of time. Ironically, as I thought I was offering these little birds a safe and welcoming environment in my own Happy Home, they were actually offering something to me –a beautiful illustration of the roles we play in God's design for a Happy Home. And so, as a nod to my houseguests and a grateful heart to our Creator, I am entitling this devotional *Cardinal Rules for a Happy Home*. May your heart also sing each day as you read and pray through the next ninety days and beyond.

Cardinal Rules for a Happy Home

"Therefore everyone who hears these words of Mine and acts on them may be compared to a wise man who built his house on the rock. And the rain fell, and the floods came, and the winds blew and slammed against that house; and yet it did not fall, for it had been founded on the rock. Everyone who hears these words of Mine and does not act on them will be like a foolish man who built his house on the sand."
Matthew 7:24-26

Everyone is building a home. Whether you are actively house-hunting or not, you are building a home. The question is how are you building and on what are you building your home? Today's scripture reminds us that a Happy Home is built on rock. When the rains of life come along, it does not fall because of the strength of the foundation on which it is built – the Lord. Psalm 94:22 says, *"But the Lord has been my stronghold, and my God the rock of my refuge."* Are you building a home that has as its foundation God, the rock of refuge?

There are different kinds of houses that people build. Some inherit a house. This is a dangerous kind of house in which to live. When you start a family, through marriage, or in raising children, you tend to bring things from your family of origin. Be careful. Inherited houses have within them old hurts, painful pasts, and unhealthy clutter. Instead, I want to encourage you to start fresh with your mate. Build your own home, so you can choose for yourself the foundation on which you will build.

We can learn something from nature, and my friends The Cardinals. After the courtship, they "house-hunt" together. At first they visit locations looking for a secure foundation on which to build, singing back and forth as if "discussing" the location. The cardinal's nest has four layers. Both male and female participate in the first layer – the foundation. This layer is sturdy and made up of the hardest and firmest twigs. The second is a leafy layer followed by a waterproofing layer of bark. Finally, they spread soft grass and crushed pine needles. They have created a sturdy home, but a soft place to land.

Is your home built on a firm foundation? Is it a place that is warm, welcoming and a soft-place to land? Incidentally, each pair of cardinals builds a new nest. They do not scavenge and occupy other birds' nests. They start fresh – confident that their nest has been well established for all who will eventually live within.

Ask the Lord to provide the foundation on which you build your Happy Home. Invite Him in, and ask that He dwell with you.

"Therefore everyone who hears these words of Mine and acts on them may be compared to a wise man who built his house on the rock. And the rain fell, and the floods came, and the winds blew and slammed against that house; and yet it did not fall, for it had been founded on the rock. Everyone who hears these words of Mine and does not act on them will be like a foolish man who built his house on the sand."
Matthew 7:24-26

I heard a story about a small boy who had attended his baby sister's dedication at church. On the ride home he cried bitterly in his car seat. His parents tried to soothe him but when the usual methods were not working the exasperated father blurted out, "Why won't you stop crying? What is wrong with you?"

Through tears, the little boy choked out, "The pastor prayed that we would be raised in a home with Christians, but I still want to live with you and mommy!"

As humorous as this story is, there are elements of truth that are not so funny. Are you building a home on wisdom, understanding, and the love of God? Are the things of God talked about and practiced routinely? Is prayer a way of life, or is it a quick blurb before a meal? Take a serious inventory of how God and Christian values are reflected in your home and to all who know you.

———————————•◦•≫≪•◦•———————————

Pray for an increased awareness to include Christian values and prayer in your daily home life.

By wisdom a house is built... **Proverbs 24:3**

Have you ever been in someone's home that has not been updated since it was built? I had an aunt who built a new home. She decorated it with the finest of fabrics, furnishings, and carpets. The windows were draped in brightly hued silks, and the chairs were covered in supple leather, fine wools, and rich velvets. The carpets were new and thick and as kids we had to take off our shoes to walk across them. My bare feet would sink down in the pile, leaving footprints as I traversed the fancy living room. I thought her house was impressive!

But as I grew older, her house did not seem as fancy. All of the same rich fabrics were there but they were faded. The sun had beaten the vibrancy out of the draperies and the chair fabrics were worn and weak in places where too many elbows had rested. And the thick, rich carpet I used to sink my toes into? Dirty, old, and matted. You see, she never remodeled. She built herself a nice house… and then left it alone.

Today's scripture tells us that wisdom builds a house. The Hebrew word for wisdom is *banah*. This word carries the connotation "to rebuild, or reconstruct." It is the same word used when Nehemiah reconstructs the wall in Jerusalem.

When we talk about building a home from a biblical perspective, we are not talking about bricks and mortar. Rather, we are talking about the principles and the essence of our family…that is our home. The old saying, "Home is where the heart is" is absolutely true. My home has always been with Jo Beth and our boys. Home is wherever they are.

Whether you are just building your home, or you have been in your home for many years, you must constantly "remodel" with wisdom. Each new day brings the opportunity to either secure our foundation in wisdom, or to ignore our house, foolishly assuming our work is done and our home is already built. When we choose to remodel and reconstruct with each new challenge or each new opportunity, we will keep our home strong, alive, and vibrantly welcoming!

Pray today for the wisdom to see the areas that need to be remodeled in your home. Pray for a keen eye and a watchful spirit to maintain a home that does not fade from neglect.

By wisdom a house is built... **Proverbs 24:3**

A few years back, we began to remodel, reconstruct, and redecorate several rooms in our home. We knew we had some updating to do to keep our home current and vibrant. Jo Beth and I easily found the things we wanted to change and devised a plan. After consulting with a decorator for some ideas, we signed off and away we went. However, we soon found out that it is the homeowners who actually endure the consequences of the remodel.

Our naïve approach was that it would not take too long, and we could easily make the changes that would greatly improve our existing house. Wrong! Remodeling developed into a much bigger undertaking than we had envisioned. I discovered four things about remodeling a home:

1. It takes a lot longer than you think it will take.
2. It costs a whole lot more than all of the estimates.
3. It takes tremendous determination and perseverance to get through.
4. It makes a bigger mess than you have been warned about.

Do you see the parallel in remodeling and reconstructing your home from a spiritual standpoint? Yesterday we talked about the evolution of updating on a daily basis. Today, we are digging into the Hebrew word *banah* – to rebuild, or reconstruct – to extrapolate more of its meaning in the passage. If a home is not constantly updated, old problems become entrenched. Therefore, remodeling will take longer and it will cost everybody involved something. There will be a mess involved as you get down to the root of the problem. However, it is worth the determination and perseverance to push through! Our home is just right for us. The remodel added comfort, beauty, and value to our home. All of the dust, money, and chaos proved to be worthwhile. We love our update, and you will too.

Prayerfully consider what needs to be remodeled in your family relationships. Ask the Lord for the patience and perseverance to deliver you through to the other side of a reconstructed relationship that is comfortable, beautiful, and worth more than pure gold!

By wisdom a house is built... **Proverbs 24:3**

Most people know the story of Adam. He was the first man God created, but because he was alone, God provided a woman for him.

What does that have to do with our scripture from Proverbs? It revolves around that little verb *banah* that we have been considering. That same verb was used in Genesis to describe what God did with Adam's rib – He built the woman by reconstructing the rib. Isn't that fascinating? I think it is a wonderful picture of marriage and of building a home. You see, the woman was reconstructed to be a helpmate and a partner for the man. However, Adam was also reconstructed. He was put back together with one less rib. As we face life together in partnership, we are reconstructed and remodeled to account for the other one God has provided.

There is wisdom in reconciling the single, independent, self-focused person with the remodeled, reconstructed person who is remade to include a spouse. Today, look at your partner and know that each of you has been supernaturally reconstructed to include the other. As God strengthens your home and your marriage through the imparted wisdom of His Spirit, take the necessary steps to yield to that reconstruction project.

Pray today for a yielded spirit to God's reconstruction of your single-self into your remodeled-self that supports and augments your spouse.

By wisdom a house is built... **Proverbs 24:3**

S TORM WARNING: Fifty percent of marriages end in divorce. This is a statistic affecting everyone reading this book. Whether you are married, single, or divorced, somewhere along the way divorce has affected your life. You may be in a marriage that is teetering on the dangerous precipice of divorce. You may be on the other side of divorce and are now single. You may be married to someone who has been divorced. Or you may be the child of divorce. Divorce is a driving and dividing force with which every marriage must contend.

Our scripture reminds us that wisdom builds a house. It is wise to know the very real threat of divorce to every marriage. The pressures on marriage are tremendous. Work, busy schedules, differing personalities, finances, and addictions are just a few of the weapons of mass-destruction that wage war on marriage. Additionally, sensualism and humanism are rampant in the culture in which we live. Loose morals and flexible standards are like having a house with loose sealant – a little air and water get in sometimes, but not much. We only begin to notice the results of the water and air when the mildew and the pests begin to overtake our home.

Do you see how dangerous the assault on a marriage can be?

God has a great building plan for marriage. It is a triangular affair. It takes a husband, a wife, and God Himself to protect a home. Think of it like a flat top roof with each spouse on one side and God laying Himself across the top to cover the entire home. *He is our shelter and our ever present help in times of trouble* (Psalm 46:1).

Divorce is a storm threat. Be on the watch. The National Weather Service often issues storm watches when the conditions are present to produce a dangerous storm. The conditions are present. Heed the warning. Do not get caught unprepared for a treacherous storm.

Pray today for the wisdom to see the areas that need to be shored up to prevent storm damage. Ask God to cover your home with His protection.

By wisdom a house is built, and by understanding it is established.
Proverbs 24:3

According to this passage, a house is established by understanding. What does the word establish mean? The Hebrew word is *kuwn*, which means, "to be firm; to be fixed; stable; securely determined; and to be directed aright." The connotation is a sense of permanence.

In Genesis, God established the very first home through the first union of man and woman. Genesis describes God's prescribed plan for marriage in the last verse of chapter 2, which says that they were naked and unashamed. Adam and Eve were totally open with each other. They were transparent with their feelings, their emotions, and their love for one another and for God. The three of them, God, Adam, and Eve, were in perfect harmony.

And then...

Sin entered the marriage. When sin entered, Adam and Eve became self-seeking, blaming, and insecure. Worse yet, they hid from God, their provider and protector. It is so important to stay transparent with your wife or husband, and with God. To keep a Happy Home— one that is stable, securely determined, and rightly directed – you must stay connected to God and your spouse. Keep sin at bay. It is not welcome in your home.

Pray today for understanding. Pray that you will be transparent with your spouse and with your Heavenly Father – open with your emotions, feelings, and love. Pray for a home established through understanding.

And he got up and went home.
Matthew 9:7

O ur scripture today is describing what a paralyzed man did after his healing. After the greatest moment in his life – where did he want to go? He wanted to go home.

Here's a test: Is your home right now a prelude to your heavenly home? Is your home a safe haven?

I remember as a child being called to the chalkboard to work a math problem in front of the class. Luckily, it was one I really understood. I knew the answer. So I went up to the board with as much confidence as a kid can have when everyone in the class is watching. As I started working the problem, I realized something had gone wrong. I must have left out one of the steps because things weren't adding up. I furiously erased and tried to retrace where I had messed up, but by now my classmates were abuzz and the teacher called time.

As I headed back to my seat, my head was hung and I could hear the snickers. Someone else was already at the chalkboard working the problem quickly and successfully. My face burned, my ears had a ringing in them, and my chalky hands were clammy.

After school, I could not wait to run into the back door of my house – home to my safe place. You see, my mother always created a welcoming environment. We did not have much in the worldly sense, but it felt warm and inviting, comfortable and safe.

The years have passed, and my failures are bigger and more intricate; but home is still that safe place for me. Jo Beth has created in our married home the same welcoming and safe haven. It is where I always want to return after failure or after triumph.

Our heavenly home will be the same – safe, welcoming, and comforting. Does that describe your home?

Pray that the Lord will bless your home and help you make it a safe and welcoming haven…a prelude to your heavenly home.

By wisdom a house is built, and by understanding it is established.
Proverbs 24:3

How understanding are you? Did you give yourself a pretty good mark? Now ask your spouse how understanding you are. What kind of mark did you receive?

Years ago, Jo Beth and I learned that to keep our home running smoothly, we would have to put our marriage second only to our relationship with God. We found that we had to continually look at situations from each other's perspective. This may seem like simplistic and generic marital advice, but have you ever tried it? It is hard to do!

This seemingly simple instruction – to look at something from your spouse's point of view – is especially difficult in the middle of a crisis. Emotions are high and reason is ready to fly out the door!

As a matter of practice, try this: Today, with each decision you make – from what to eat for breakfast to what you watch on TV tonight – do what you think your spouse would prefer. I believe you will be amazed to see the positive effect praying and seeking to establish your home with true understanding for one another will produce.

Pray today for understanding. Pray for the supernatural ability to think and feel like your spouse. Pray for eyes to see, ears to hear, and a heart to feel another's perspective. Pray that true understanding will establish your house.

By wisdom a house is built, and by understanding it is established.
Proverbs 24:3

There are so few things that are permanent these days. We live in a culture that expends anything that does not hold our immediate attention. We like fast food, immediate hot water, direct TV, instant messaging, and the latest fashion trends.

Is your home and your marriage in that same category? Has your spouse become dispensable? Is home a place where you shower and change, or do you want to dwell there?

I can tell you one thing that is permanent – established – in my life is my marriage. Jo Beth is stuck with me, and I am with her, and we would not have it any other way. Because we have asked God to dwell in us and with us, we have established a permanence that is unwavering.

Let me be clear: we have a good marriage, but it is not because we are good at it. We have made a commitment to ask God for protection and for wisdom in building our home. With wisdom comes discernment. Understanding is the practical application of discernment. I pray daily for it. Once God gives me the ability to discern what Jo Beth is feeling and needing, I am in a better position to be understanding. Through understanding each other, we have established a marriage that sizzles with fun, delight, passion, and compassion. When we are together, we are home!

Pray today for understanding. Ask God to give you the ability to discern what your spouse needs and feels.

By wisdom a house is built, and by understanding it is established; and by knowledge the rooms are filled with all precious and pleasant riches.
Proverbs 24:3-4

We have a friend who had it all: beauty, charisma, intelligence, and great wealth. She was married to her college sweetheart, and boy were they a great couple. They had it all – fantastic clothes, fancy cars, summer homes, winter get-aways, and three of the smartest, best-looking, talented children you ever saw. Their home seemed to fit the Proverbs 24:4 description of a home filled with precious and pleasant riches.

Except that it wasn't. The verse tells us that by knowledge the rooms are filled with wonderful things. The Hebrew word for knowledge is defined as having both wisdom and discernment, or understanding. Knowledge is the culmination of what we get when we have built a house through wisdom and established it through understanding. We get to experience the pleasantness, and precious riches ensue.

My friend was sadly like Solomon, the writer of today's passage. Solomon knew the secret to a Happy Home. He had the wisdom, he had the understanding, but he did not apply it in the end. Same with my friend. She let sin seep into her life and though her home was filled with valuable adornments, her riches were not pleasant.

Today her home no longer houses what was once precious to her: her husband and her children. What it housed instead was a meth lab. The FBI has since shut that down. Her wealth is still intact, but her precious and pleasant riches are now gone. Sin came knocking and she opened the door.

Pray today for knowledge and that God will empower you to apply wisdom and understanding. Pray against any temptations that would keep precious and pleasant riches from filling your home.

By wisdom a house is built, and by understanding it is established; and by knowledge the rooms are filled with all precious and pleasant riches.
Proverbs 24:3-4

Many years ago, the phone rang late at night. My heart pounded. A quick mental inventory gave me the comfort that all of my boys, who were kids at the time, were home. I picked up the phone and received the news that there was black smoke billowing from the new house we were building. I threw on some clothes and shoes and drove over to the site. As reported, black smoke was billowing up into the midnight sky. A tragic feeling washed over me.

As I stood and looked at what had been our dream home, my heart sank. We had borrowed and stretched ourselves to have this house. We wanted it for the boys. I wanted it for Jo Beth, and she wanted it for me. The attention to detail, the cost, and the passion we had exerted were gone in a puff of smoke.

Then a wave of the Holy Spirit's comfort washed over me. I will never forget it. It was the knowledge that my riches were still safely tucked in their beds, out of the line of this fire. My precious and pleasant riches filled the rooms of my house and my heart. What Jo Beth and I had established as a family was untouched by the black smoke of this tragedy.

Ask your Heavenly Father to fill your marriage and your family with precious, pleasant, and untouchable riches.

By wisdom a house is built, and by understanding it is established; and by knowledge the rooms are filled with all precious and pleasant riches.
Proverbs 24:3-4

Going back to the original language often gives us insight into studying Scripture. The Hebrew word for *filled* carries with it the connotation of something that can hold no more. It is literally so full that it is running over. This same word was used for storm clouds that were so full they had to drop rain. Another use for this word in the Bible is in its Greek form, which refers to being drunk, or filled with wine to the point of drunkenness.

This is the picture the writer is describing in Proverbs 24:4. Our home is so full of pleasant and precious things that it is saturated. We are not looking at a glass that has some water in it – we are looking at a glass that has water spilling over the top! As we combine wisdom and understanding, true knowledge will emerge and our home will be overflowing with precious and pleasant things.

Pray today for knowledge that produces the overflowing and saturation of precious and pleasant riches in your home, your heart, and your family.

For the Lord gives wisdom; from His mouth come knowledge and understanding.
Proverbs 2:6

Y ou have prayed for wisdom. You have prayed for understanding. You have prayed for knowledge. Now what? Many of us pray these prayers and hope for the best. But today's verse gives us hope and certainty. Proverbs 2:6 clearly tells us where these attributes come from – they come from the Lord.

As King Solomon expressed in Proverbs, the Lord gives wisdom. As we ask the Lord for His wisdom, an added bonus emerges: knowledge and understanding. These are gifts only the Lord can provide. When we seek wisdom for our family, God imparts direction and comprehension for every situation we face.

Pray today with confidence: the Lord gives wisdom. It is not up to you!

Ask the Lord to impart wisdom, knowledge, and understanding to you for your family. Name a situation you are facing and ask specifically that He give you wisdom in that area.

Unless the Lord builds the house, They labor in vain who build it.
Psalm 127:1

We all have seen the results of a do-it-yourself project that should have been handled by a professional. As tempting as it is to save a little money on the front end, the lack of experience and training usually results in a much more costly and time-consuming mess. This is how it is when we usurp God's position within our family structure. As a husband and father, I know I can give Jo Beth and the boys my very best effort and still fall short in some areas, and our home life will fall into disrepair. My family will suffer even if I am trying my best. There will always be a new challenge that one of my sons faces, or a tough call to make at church, or something Jo Beth will need from me that I am not sure how to give. Slowly but surely I will become overwhelmed if I rely on my own strength and "building" techniques.

Psalm 127:1 states this clearly, but I encourage you to let this knowledge give you comfort as it does me. In the context of your family, you are not alone in the "home-building project!" The Heavenly Father is the builder. When you enlist Him to build your home, you have the Master Carpenter.

Wisdom is not up to you. Understanding cannot be attained by sheer will, and knowledge is merely a compilation of facts unless inspired by the Lord.

So relax. You are not called to a do-it-yourself homebuilding project. Far from it. In fact, if you try to labor alone, your efforts will be in vain.

Pray today to release your home to the Master. Ask Him to step in and help build and fortify your house by His might and His Spirit.

Can the Ethiopian change his skin or the leopard his spots? Then you also can do good who are accustomed to doing evil.
Jeremiah 13:23

My wife and I love to go to Hawaii. I usually pack in advance in anticipation of the perfect weather and beautiful scenery. I take things with me that I would not wear at home, including shorts, loud tropical-printed shirts, and sunscreen. I look forward to the mouthwatering tropical fruit and seventy-two-degree weather. I enjoy golf in the morning, reading in a shaded hammock at noon, exercise in the evening, and then a delicious dinner right at sunset with Jo Beth beside me enjoying everything as much as I do!

Imagine that not too long into my flight to Hawaii we hit turbulence. The result: we are re-routed and land in Switzerland where it is freezing! JoBeth and I get off the plane, and no one around is speaking English. My tropical shirt is too thin, and I am chilled to the bone. Jo Beth is unhappy with the results and begins to complain. So what should we do?

First, I would make sure we get some warm clothes. Next, I would say, "Honey, I think we would enjoy this more if we learn to ski." Next, depending on how long it looks like we are going to be in Switzerland, we might consult a professional and begin to learn a new language.

Sound reasonable? Many couples approach marriage this way. They find themselves leaving for a fantasy trip to a tropical island, but run into turbulence and end up in a much different terrain. However, once there, they refuse to adapt. Instead, they stay miserably cold in their tropical clothing, decline to learn any skills for the new terrain, and are overtaken by an avalanche of marital problems.

Your marriage can weather turbulence and adapt to a new and unexpected climate. The key is to be willing to change. Our scripture illustrates that some things we cannot change, like a leopard cannot change his spots. But the very next verse says we can be changed as a person. We can turn from what we are doing and "do good." Are you willing to turn and make the changes that your current marital climate needs?

Ask for the Lord to give you the wisdom, knowledge, and understanding to turn from what is not right in your relationships and to make the changes to adapt to whatever climate you are facing. Ask the Lord to make the mountains you are facing into "mountain-top" experiences of victory.

Then the Philistines seized him, gouged out his eyes and took him down to Gaza.
Binding him with bronze shackles, they set him to grinding grain in the prison.
But the hair on his head began to grow again after it had been shaved.
Judges 16:21-22 NIV

S amson had been blinded, bound, and imprisoned because of his sin. He had forsaken his people, his family, and his God for the momentary pleasure that Delilah provided. As you may remember, his strength was in his hair. After seducing him, Delilah cut his hair and he was captured. BUT…his hair began to grow back!

This is a beautiful picture of what God can do in our families. Even though we may have become blinded to our mates and fallen into a dungeon of sin, heartache, resistance, and coldness, seemingly grinding away the time…God can renew our strength and effect real change.

"I married the wrong person."
"Our backgrounds are too different."
"We married at the wrong time."
"He never hears me."
"My marriage is stagnant."
"Our sex life isn't satisfying."
"I am bored."

All of these are common phrases and common excuses for avoiding change in your marriage. YOU CANNOT CHANGE YOUR MATE. True. But you can change yourself, and you can change your marriage.

If any of these thoughts has ever flitted across the theater of your mind, stop the show. Instead, begin to take real action. Start today and replace these statements with the following:

"I am going to do something about my marriage."
"I am going to follow God's plan for marriage."
"I am going to seek change in MYSELF."
"With God's grace, all things can be made new again."

Pray that God will give you renewed strength and desire to move toward change and out of the bondage that can threaten a Happy Home, and that He will empower you with the Spirit of the Heavenly Father.

Be angry, and yet do not sin; do not let the sun go down on your anger,
and do not give the Devil an opportunity.
Ephesians 4:26-27

Through the years, I have performed countless wedding ceremonies. Almost without exception, I have been tempted to change the vows from "Love, Honor, and Obey," to "Love, Honor, and FORGIVE."

Christian psychiatrist Dr. Leslie Brant says that the divorce rate would decrease by half if forgiveness were as much a part of marriage as the conjugal bed.

God created male and female, and He created them to be different. Physically our differences are obvious. Why is it then that we are so surprised that emotionally we are completely different as well?

When we disappoint our mate, it is often because we fail to take into account our differences. Men, we are especially culpable here. Women at least try to get their minds around what makes a man tick. However, without prayer and perseverance, we guys fail miserably.

With all of these differences, the best and only way to live in harmony with the opposite sex is to implement forgiveness as an everyday exercise. The beauty of forgiveness is that it builds a bridge for the other to walk across. Without it, the divide can become cold, dark, and lonely.

Forgive your mate daily, and the reward will be a deep, meaningful, and joyful marriage that sizzles!

Ask the Lord to bring to mind anything that needs to be forgiven in your marriage. Pray that with His help, you will be able to forgive and create a marriage that is grace-oriented.

Do not let the sun go down on your anger, and do not give the Devil an opportunity.
Ephesians 4:26-27

There is no marriage advice better than this verse. Do not let the sun go down on your anger. Period. Time is very important here. Paul, the writer of Ephesians, is cautioning about letting time go by when we are angry. He says to deal with the issue before it gets dark and you go to sleep at night. As time goes by, everything calms down and the immediacy of the argument wanes. But the importance of forgiveness wanes as well. When an argument is unresolved, a cold bitterness can glaze over the heart and numb us to each other. It is vital to keep a tender heart.

Start this practice today. Resolve your issues before you go to bed tonight. This is a simple practice which will garner enormous results for the health and vitality of your marriage!

Ask the Lord to facilitate a resolution to any anger or resentment that you have today. Pray that you will have a forgiving heart and that the sun will set today on a clean heart and a clean slate.

O my dove, in the clefts of the rock, in the secret place of the steep pathway, let me see your form. Let me hear your voice; for your voice is sweet, and your form is lovely. Catch the foxes for us, the little foxes that are ruining the vineyards, while our vineyards are in blossom. **Song of Solomon 2:14-15**

Song of Solomon celebrates the intimacy, love, and romance of marriage. As a wise lover and a godly husband, Solomon writes about his wife with tenderness, adoration, and awe. But right in the middle of all of these loving descriptions, he inserts a peculiar phrase: *"Catch the foxes for us, the little foxes that are ruining the vineyards while our vineyards are in blossom."* Solomon is alluding to the fact that even with the best passion and attentiveness between a husband and wife, little things can creep in and begin to eat away at the marriage.

The truth of the matter is that most divorces are filed under the designation, "irreconcilable differences." These differences are the culmination of small annoyances that grow. If irritations are not forgiven daily, unforgiveness, bitterness, and disdain creep in and create strong fortresses behind which the husband and wife seclude themselves. Each spouse takes refuge behind a fortress of his or her own design.

Do not let the "little foxes" go unnoticed. Forgive each other daily. No matter how seemingly insignificant, if something irritates you forgive it. Nothing is too small for the enemy to use as a brick in your fortress wall.

———————————— ✸ ————————————

Ask the Lord to bring to mind anything that needs to be forgiven in your marriage. Pray that even the small things will be brought into the light of His grace, and you will be a forgiving spouse.

Do not grieve the Holy Spirit of God, by whom you were sealed for the day of redemption. Let all bitterness, wrath, anger, clamor, and slander be put away from you, along with all malice. Be kind to one another, tender-hearted, forgiving each other, just as God in Christ also has forgiven you.

Ephesians 4:30-32

An argument between a husband and wife develops in stages. Do you recognize any of the following?

Stage I is the wounded heart. At this stage, each side feels hurt. This stage usually is expressed with tears, anger, or that whipped-dog look. However, if we do not let the sun go down on our anger, we'll come through the wounded heart stage. When we forgive, there is healing; but many times we move to Stage II.

Stage II is the cold heart. We make this transition from wounded heart to cold heart seamlessly. To keep the peace, we may act nice, considerate, and overtly fine; yet inside, our heart has become cold and walled off – less vulnerable to another wound.

Then there is Stage III, the hardened heart. In Ephesians 4, Paul tells us how dangerous the hardened heart is. He begins by warning us not to let the sun go down on our wrath. He says, "Do not grieve the Holy Spirit." The Holy Spirit is grieved when we have a hardened, impenetrable heart. We no longer demonstrate fruit of the Spirit: kindness, goodness, gentleness, etc. Instead, we have become firm and set in our indignation: we know we are right; we know we were wronged. In this stage, it becomes difficult to pray. We are so bitter and resolute in our position that even admitting weakness to God seems impossible.

Stage III is not as difficult as Stage IV, the apathetic heart. Psychiatrist Rollo May says that the opposite of love is not hate. The opposite of love is apathy. Do you see the progression? I'm wounded; I'm cold – calculating; I'm hard; and finally, I'm apathetic. I don't care anymore. I don't have the energy to hate; I'm just paralyzed. I'm out of business. Love has died, and I don't feel anything.

Recognize the stages. Tomorrow we will see how to reverse the stages…no matter how far your heart has gone.

Pray that the Lord would help you resolve any anger and move your relationship into the realm of forgiveness and healing.

Do not grieve the Holy Spirit of God, by whom you were sealed for the day of redemption. Let all bitterness, wrath, anger, clamor, and slander be put away from you, along with all malice. Be kind to one another, tender-hearted, forgiving each other, just as God in Christ also has forgiven you.

Ephesians 4:30-32

Here is a review of the stages of an argument. With each stage, the danger to your marriage increases.

Stage I - Wounded Heart

Stage II - Cold Heart

Stage III - Hardened Heart

Stage IV - Apathetic Heart

The good news is that these stages can be reversed! Here is how:

1. Go to the foot of the Cross. There is level ground there. Remember, He died for both of you.

2. Apprehend the fresh forgiveness and the cleansing of God in Jesus Christ. Claim it for yourself. Be forgiven and healed for your part of the problem.

3. Surrender your will to God. Yes – do it! Say, "I am willing to forgive." Your feelings may not change immediately. This is a discipline, a willing act of participation on your part.

4. Communicate with your spouse. Confess your part.

5. Now, forgive yourself.

Pray through each step listed above. Start at the Cross, the place from which grace and mercy flow.

*Be kind to one another, tender-hearted, forgiving each other,
just as God in Christ also has forgiven you.*
Ephesians 4:32

What is forgiveness? We talk a lot about it, but do we truly understand what forgiveness looks like?

To understand what forgiveness is, let's first look at what it is not. Forgiveness is NOT saying, "Oh, it's alright." It is NOT saying, "Oh, let's just forget about it." It is NOT saying, "Let's drop it...we don't have to talk about it anymore." Forgiveness is NOT painting over something, ignoring it, or putting on rose-colored glasses to view a wrong in a more favorable light.

Instead, forgiveness costs something. It is taking the pain, the shame, and the guilt of another person and burying it within yourself. Forgiveness always involves a cross. It is taking the shabbiness of someone else and coming to terms with it. It is painful. There is no such thing as cheap grace. It is exceedingly expensive to forgive.

Now we can understand the value of a forgiving spouse. The marriage built on forgiveness is a tremendous thing to behold...but even better to experience!

Ask the Lord to give you the right approach and correct understanding of true forgiveness. Ask Him to equip you to forgive others as He forgave you.

All this is from God, who reconciled us to Himself through Christ and gave us the ministry of reconciliation: that God was reconciling the world to Himself in Christ, not counting people's sins against them, and He has committed to us the message of reconciliation.
II Corinthians 5:18-19

I know of a man who served his country in World War II. Shortly after he was married, he shipped out, leaving behind his sweetheart, a godly young woman. She supported him with prayers and encouraging letters throughout the war. When he returned safely, it seemed like their life was off to a perfect start.

Until...

One day while sorting through and cleaning her husband's belongings, she found a stash of love letters that were not from her. He had begun an affair with a woman in Europe. This woman had also sent him love letters during the war. His wife was devastated. All of her prayers, all of her letters, all of her trust now seemed stained, defiled. Her heart was broken, but she said nothing.

One afternoon, her husband heard her sobs and walked in to see what was going on. When he saw she was in distress, he hurried to comfort her, but he stopped short. As he looked at her face, something told him her anguish would not be soothed by him. He recalls looking up and seeing her arms spread wide in anguish of the soul. From across the room, he could see the shadow she cast upon the wall. It was that of a cross. He recalls, "I knew in that moment that my sweet, innocent wife was being crucified because of my sins."

He fell on his face and cried out to God, "Oh, what have I done? What have I done?" He does not know how long he was in that position, his remorse was so intense, but he felt his wife's hands on his head. She kissed the crown of his head, and said, "Oh Bill, I forgive you, I forgive you." Bill describes another voice he heard. "My son, I forgive you too. Now go and sin no more."

Pray for the conviction of the Holy Spirit to prompt repentance and to be empowered to forgive others when wronged.

Love is patient, love is kind. It does not envy, it does not boast, it is not proud. It does not dishonor others, it is not self-seeking, it is not easily angered, and it keeps no record of wrongs. **I Corinthians 13:4-5 NIV**

The story from yesterday's devotional did not end with that climactic scene of true remorse and forgiveness. You see, the wife forgave in the moment, but her heart had been wounded. A strange and bitter fascination began to grow in regard to those letters. She stowed them in a secret drawer and forgot about them. Except…except for times when she was hurt, or angry, or lonely. Then she would ruminate on the letters. She would remind herself that she had the goods on her husband – proof of his sin, and proof of her great act of forgiveness.

One day as she was reading her Bible, she read I Corinthians 13, "*…keeps no record of wrongs.*" She knew the Lord was dealing with her heart and wanted to heal her hurt, but to be healed, she had to act in obedience. She was keeping a record of wrongs, making her guilty of a sin as well. So she hurried to her secret drawer and pulled out the yellowed sheaf of papers. She went to the fireplace and tossed them in. She describes watching the paper curl up and disappear within seconds.

She recalled thinking, "Christ forgives us that quickly." However, eeriness fell over the room. For years she had given Satan territory within her marriage – a record of wrongs, bitterness, and unforgiveness. She said a Satanic sounding voice taunted her saying, "You are destroying the evidence! Your husband will be totally free of his egregious acts against you!"

Aloud she answered, "Thank God, that is exactly what I am doing. Forgiving love keeps no records of wrongs!"

Search your heart today and ask the Lord to bring to light any records of wrong you have filed away in the secret drawer of your heart. Bring them to the light of true forgiveness. Pray for the ability to forgive and be free as you set your loved one free from the record that you have secretly kept.

Put to death, therefore, whatever belongs to your earthly nature: sexual immorality, impurity, lust, evil desires and greed, which is idolatry. Because of these, the wrath of God is coming. **Colossians 3:5-6 NIV**

There are many enemies of a Happy Home. Some are outside the home, but I want to concentrate on the enemies within the home. We have more ability to conquer these, because we have let them in ourselves. The first enemy I want us to consider is idolatry. This enemy can sneak up on us and become firmly entrenched before we realize it.

I have known many well-intended families who have worked very hard to provide for their mates, children, and loved-ones. However, when the desire to provide and achieve begins to outshine the desire and commitment to serve the Lord, idolatry has entered the camp.

Weariness can set in, and we begin to skip church. You know the subtle ways we reverse priorities. The kids wake up on Sunday morning. You are tired, they are tired, and it is raining. You decide it is easier to sleep in, have a leisurely morning, and forgo church.

Or, perhaps success has provided a fancy new boat or a lake house. You begin to skip church because the weekend gives you the best opportunity to enjoy your riches.

However, Monday rolls around and the kids don't want to go to school because…it's raining! Or they want to go ride in the boat. But work and school are the major priority. We can't miss work and we can't miss school! Do you see how we can confuse kids when we do not prioritize correctly?

Anything that takes precedence over God becomes an idol. Are you safe within your home, or is there an idol creeping into your camp?

Pray for the Lord to secure your home. Ask the Lord to bring to mind any areas that may become idolatrous and confess them aloud. Pray today for a renewed commitment to the Lord within your home.

Whoever commits adultery with a woman lacks understanding;
He who does so destroys his own soul.
Proverbs 6:32 NKJV

As we resume our focus on the enemies within the home, I want us to consider one that is gaining tremendous ground and tearing marriages and families apart: infidelity. Men, guard your homes. Take proactive steps to keep this enemy out. Set ground rules for yourself; do not make your wife set the rules for you. Christian men especially need to be on guard. The divorce rate is statistically as high for Christian marriages as it is for all others. Here are some rules of thumb that help establish a moat of safety around your home, your marriage, and your relationship with God:

1. Never allow yourself to be alone with a woman other than your wife. No exceptions. Look at exceptions as spies from the enemy's camp.

2. Do not discuss your wife with other women…ever. Often we think we are seeking advice, but instead, we are betraying our vows to love, honor, and respect.

3. Keep no secrets. Share email and cell phone passwords. Transparency and honesty are foundational for godly intimacy.

4. Be in the habit of giving non-sexual touch daily. Women need this and thrive on tenderhearted connection.

5. Do not go to bed angry…always make amends before the sun goes down.

6. Pray together every day. Intimacy with the Lord inspires intimacy with each other.

The home is a target. Take steps to guard your home, your marriage, and your family from the sin of infidelity. Adultery comes in all shapes and sizes. Each brings disaster, heartache, and despair. Keep your home and marriage fortified, and know how to spot an enemy attack before it gets too close to home.

Men, pray for the Lord to secure your home. Ask the Lord to equip you to make wise choices, and to take proactive steps to protect you and your family from the sin of infidelity.

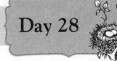

You shall not commit adultery.
Exodus 20:14

Increasingly in our culture, women are the ones who stray from their marriage vows. Traditionally, a couple would seek counsel because the husband had strayed, while the wife struggled to accept her contrite husband back into her heart and their home. But sexual infidelity from wives is on the rise. Why? Often I hear the same answer: "My husband was emotionally unavailable to me." "I was emotionally starved out of the relationship." "I met someone who really gets me."

There is no excuse for infidelity. However, men need to be charged with the leadership of the home. We are commanded to love our wives as Christ loved the church: with tenderness, affection, and intimacy. Women need affection and emotional intimacy. Men, make that sacrifice for your wife, even if it feels unnatural.

A strong armor must be placed around the sanctity of marriage. Women as well as men must take a proactive stance in guarding their homes against the enemy. Women:

1. Never allow yourself to be alone with a man other than your husband. No exceptions. Look at exceptions as spies from the enemy's camp.

2. Do not discuss your husband with other men…ever. Often we think we are seeking advice, but instead, we are betraying our vows to love, honor, and respect.

3. Do not air your disappointments with your husband to your friends. There is no room in a marriage for a girls' committee. If you need advice, seek godly counsel.

4. Keep no secrets. Share email and cell phone passwords. Transparency and honesty are foundational for godly intimacy.

5. Do not go to bed angry…always make amends before the sun goes down.

6. Pray together daily; intimacy with the Lord inspires intimacy with each other.

Stay strong, focus on each other and God, and be on guard against the seemingly innocent tactics of the enemy.

Women, pray for the Lord to secure your home. Ask the Lord to equip you to make wise choices, and to take proactive steps to protect you and your family from the sin of infidelity.

You shall not commit adultery.
Exodus 20:14

Infidelity can be of a non-sexual nature. Be on your guard against two different types of non-sexual infidelity. One is the emotional affair, which we will examine today.

Men, when your wife is tired, overworked, up to her ears in thankless tasks and does not take the time to make you feel like the king of the home, there will always be a kind, compassionate listener who "gets you." Or there will be a fun-loving girl who simply enjoys life and seems to need no emotional collateral from you. Be warned! This is the beginning of a treacherous and slippery slope. Making an emotional or fun-loving connection with someone other than your wife amounts to an emotional affair. Stay away from it.

Husbands: Your wife is your confidant. Give her grace when she is tired, and go the extra mile to serve her when you are the one who actually desires the attention. This is how Christ loved the church.

Women, likewise be on your guard against neglecting your husband because of your own personal distractions, or worse – because you feel like he neglects you first. A more sensitive man who notices you and understands you may be available, but he is your enemy. Do not let his compassionate words and attentions fool you. Your marriage is at risk.

Wives: Your husband should be your priority. Give him your full attention when you see each other at the end of the day. This signals respect, which makes him feel loved.

Serve one another sacrificially. Keep your marriage and your partner as your highest priority, second only to Christ. Selfishness within the home opens the door to emotional infidelity.

Ask the Lord to help each of you sacrificially serve each other. He alone will meet all of your other needs.

He who finds a wife finds a good thing and obtains favor from the LORD.
Proverbs 18:22

As we discussed yesterday, infidelity can be of a non-sexual nature. Today we are going to look at disloyalty within the home. Women, this is an area that can easily entrap you. Because of God's design, women are more natural emotional connectors. They are designed to nurture and nest. This is not a sexist statement; in fact, it is a strength with which God equipped women – to connect. Women make deep and meaningful connections much more readily than men. Research proves that women have closer and longer sustained friendships than men.

Often this seemingly innocent fact can provide a fertile place for disloyalty to grow within a marriage. When you recount to an audience of "gal-pals" all of the drama within your marriage, you break the sacredness of your matrimony. Likewise, treating a group of friends as a committee with voting rights brings more than two people into the holy and mysterious bond of a Christ-centered marriage. This behavior amounts to a lack of faithfulness within your marriage.

Men are prone to the same disloyalty – it just looks different. When men confide the intimate details of their marriage to one another, they have been unfaithful. Men, complaining about your wife will always garner sympathy from the single guys you know, but guess what? They are usually looking for someone just like your wife. She is your treasure, your very great reward from God. Honor your vows and protect your privacy.

Disloyalty within a marriage can appear innocent at first. Be on guard. Your treasure is always at risk when you allow others to peer behind your protected walls.

Pray today for the wisdom to protect your home from disloyalty. Pray that God will lead you to wise counsel should there be need for a third party to speak into your marriage.

Honor marriage, and guard the sacredness of sexual intimacy between wife and husband. God draws a firm line against casual and illicit sex.
Hebrews 13:4 MSG

I want to talk about a nuclear bomb that can destroy a home: adultery. We all know that sex is a powerful force. It can be a beautiful servant, or a demanding master. It is therefore important to understand that sex is a gift from God for husbands and wives. It was created in the mind and genius of God Himself. The idea that sex is wrong is not biblical; but the idea that sex is open to any and to all is not biblical either.

It is sex that draws the man to the woman and the woman to the man. It is the magnetism, the chemistry that begins the attraction. Within the context of the family, it is this chemistry that drives the man to work, to pursue, and to provide. Likewise, it is within this sexual context of the marriage that the woman can express her femininity, her nurturing, and her loving side. This brings children into being. A nuclear family is created.

Within this godly family, sexual motivation is properly channeled, and within this intimate husband and wife relationship, a wholesome and dynamic structure is created.

An atom has a nucleus with protons, electrons, and neutrons, held together by an electrical force. If anything splits that atom, there is nuclear fission: an atomic bomb.

So it is in the home. It is the sexual electricity and magnetism that keeps a family together in an intimate, loving, and exciting way. But if something splits that, or if the energy is spread out, destruction follows. Be diligent to guard your home against a nuclear attack. Safeguard and cherish the beautiful gift of sex within your marriage and protect your Happy Home.

Give thanks for the beautiful gift of sexual intimacy. Ask the Lord to protect and guard your home and your marriage from destructive forces.

Honor your father and mother (which is the first commandment with a promise), so that it may be well with you, and that you may live long on the earth. Fathers, do not provoke your children to anger, but bring them up in the discipline and instruction of the Lord.

Ephesians 6:2-4

Another enemy from within the home is overly harsh discipline. The word discipline comes from the word disciple, which means "one who follows in the way; imitates one's example." Obviously when we see the word, we think of Jesus' disciples. They in fact embodied that definition of "following in the way" of Jesus, and imitating His example. Did you know that we as parents are setting that example for our children – good or bad?

The basic tenet of discipline within the Christian home is *"Honor your father and mother"* – which is the first commandment with a promise – *"so that it may go well with you, and that you may enjoy long life on the earth."*

This commandment is so vital that God attached a promise to it. Paul adds a corrective element to the familiar commandment. *"Fathers, do not provoke your children to anger, but bring them up in the discipline and instruction of the Lord."*

What does this mean? It means that discipline can be so intense, inflexible, and carried out with such self-righteous indignation that it does not do what it was intended to do: to teach and to train. Instead, it can break a child's spirit. Unyielding discipline can deteriorate the character of a child. It can suppress joy and entice bitterness and resentment.

Parents, discipline must be exacted with love and with limits. The bottom line is this – set a good example for your little disciples. Correct them with love as Jesus does with you.

Ask the Lord to help you discipline with love and within limits. Confess a need for the Lord's intervention in both the way you discipline, and in the way you honor your own parents.

All of us like sheep have gone astray; each of us has turned to his own way.
Isaiah 53:6

Our country and our culture celebrate independence. We laud those who go off on their own and seek no one else's approval as they reach for new heights of accomplishment, freedom, or popularity. But the Bible looks at life from a very different perspective.

The Bible teaches that we all like sheep have gone astray. All have gone astray, and that includes you and me! This verse not only declares that each of us strays, but also explains how we stray: by turning to our own way. That is what I call selfish independence, which may be the greatest problem in marriages today.

Sin is not adultery. Adultery is an act of sin. Sin is not murder. Murder is an act of sin. Sin is not abuse. Abuse is an act of sin. We commit adultery because we ourselves are sinful. We turn to our own way, and independent of our vows and our covenant, we commit a selfish act to meet our own needs. When someone kills another human being, he is doing what his flesh feels like doing – independent of the laws of the nation and the laws of God. It is selfish independence. When a raging man verbally abuses his wife or children, he is blowing off his own steam and scalding everyone else in the process – selfish independence.

So at the root of sin is a firmly planted sense of selfish independence. In marriage, we have two sinful people coming together. If both exert their selfish independence, the "oneness" will die. Sin and selfishness by their very definitions are destructive. Before egregious sin enters your marriage, take a good hard look at yourself. Are you still trying to be independent? If so, confess your selfish tendency to your spouse and to the Lord.

The antidote for selfish independence is interdependence, which is a state in which we are dependent on other people in our lives for certain things, and other people are dependent on us as well. This is a healthy "give-take" relationship.

There is a freedom in interdependence that no amount of selfish independence provides. Declare today *Inter*dependence Day in your home!

Pray for interdependence within your home and total dependence upon the Lord.

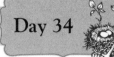

Day 34

All of us like sheep have gone astray; each of us has turned to his own way.
Isaiah 53:6

Every sermon I preach begins with the same prayer, "Lord, You speak and let me get out of Your way." As humble as that may sound, it comes from desperation, not from humility. You see, long before I get to church on Sunday morning, I have already been in a battle. As I prepare for a sermon, I spend days in prayer, meditation, and study. However, Sunday morning is game day, and I have to physically get myself to work. So, I come out of that reverent mode that I've been in all week and begin the seemingly mindless tasks of getting dressed, eating breakfast, and driving to church. It is in these practicalities that my flesh takes over. You would think that from all that time spent seeking the Lord, I would be radiant! But as the verse says, I turn to my own way…and often, become a bear! Just ask Jo Beth. I can never seem to find what I need, from shaving cream to the right tie. So I start looking for a place to cast blame, and it usually lands on my wife.

I begin to think about how she serves so many people and probably forgets about me. Poor me, poor neglected me. If one of my sons needed shaving cream, I dare say she would even drive to Dallas to take it to her first-born. "What about me?" I silently ponder.

I confess this to you to show you two things: First, be aware that we are tempted and tried by the devil in ways and at times that don't make sense – like Sunday mornings. Secondly, respond like Jo Beth. Even during my huffing and puffing, she is kind, generous, and non-reactive. She is the hardest person in the world to fight with. She gives me a wide berth, lets the Lord convict me, and selflessly meets my needs even when I am acting grumpy and selfish.

I have learned a valuable lesson from my wife about how to serve selflessly. We are now over fifty years into our marriage, and my heart's desire is to out-serve her. It really is. I want to do more for her than she does for me, but it is hard because she is so good at it. But that's a good problem to have. I pray you will have this problem, too.

Ask the Lord to fill you with the desire to serve Him first, and to out-serve your mate today and always.

We know love by this, that He laid down His life for us;
and we ought to lay down our lives for the brethren.
I John 3:16

O ver the years, people have asked me, "Pastor, when do you know that you are ready to get married?" Or parents will have a son or a daughter who is seriously dating and they approach me and ask, "What age should a person be when he or she gets married?"

What is that magical age at which you no longer go by separate names, and you become Mr. and Mrs. I-Do?

I have the answer. You are ready to get married when:

- You are mature enough to know who you are without confusion.

- You are mature enough to settle with one person forever without wavering.

- You are mature enough to give more than you receive.

- You are mature enough to share more than you keep.

- You are mature enough to love and to be loved without reservation.

- You are mature enough to invest sufficient energy to cultivate a life other than your own.

If you can say, "I am," to all of those conditions, then you are ready to say, "I do."

If you are already married, re-read the list. If you cannot in good-conscience say that you are actively doing each of those things, start today. It is never too late to redo your "I do."

Continue to grow and to ask the Lord to help you mature your relationship into the blessed union He intends it to be.

Pray that God will mature you relationally. Ask for His help and His guidance to give you the ability to mature in the areas that you are lacking, and to strengthen the areas where you are already growing.

We all like sheep have gone astray; each of us has turned to our own way.
Isaiah 53:6 NIV

Today I am going to ask you to take what I call the 30/7 Challenge. It is especially effective for marriages that are in the midst of a storm. Is your marriage worth 30 minutes a day for 7 days? Let me assure you that divorce will cost you far more than the next 7 days, so I encourage you to give this a try.

Find a place to be together and undistracted for 30 minutes each day for the next 7 days. Bring your Bible and a clock. Pull up two chairs to face each other and sit. Start the clock – thirty minutes divided into 5-minute increments. Note that you will stay completely silent for the first three segments!

1st five minutes: Think about what the future would be like without that person.

MEN: Imagine coming home to a house without her feminine touch. Night after night your children will grow and change without you. Proven fact – if you remarry, you are 3 times more likely to get divorced again. If you have someone in mind, know that statistics prove you will be in this position with her.

WOMEN: Statistics are higher that you will not get remarried. However, if you do, you are much more likely to repeat this pattern with a new husband.

2nd five minutes: Pray, "Lord, what is my contributing factor to this turmoil?" Let God speak to you about you not your mate.

3rd five minutes: Think about your children. Do not rationalize that your children will not be affected; you are also affecting their future homes.

4th five minutes: Open your Bibles to I Corinthians 13. Take turns reading it back and forth to each other. She may start, "Love is patient." He then reads, "Love is kind." And so on…

5th five minutes: Each of you share a memory of happier times: when your child was born, or when you first met. Recall times when you pulled together. Recall positive aspects of past events.

6th five minutes: Be still again. Rest in the fact that God has a plan. He is in the business of healing.

Will you take the challenge?

Ask the Lord to help you face the challenges in your marriage. Ask for fresh understanding and a productive 7 day challenge.

Husbands, love your wives, just as Christ also
loved the church and gave Himself up for her.
Ephesians 5:25

Years ago I heard a story of an old man who was having trouble with "the Missus," as he put it. They decided to talk to their pastor. While in his office, the wife sat quietly crying while the husband looked uncomfortable and awkward. Finally the pastor was able to ask, "Ma'am, what is on your heart? Why are you so sad?"

Through tears, she wailed, "My husband doesn't love me anymore."

To which the pastor asked him, "Is what she fears true?"

The grumpy man looked agitated, "Of course not! She's always saying that."

The pastor gently asked, "Well, what have you done to reassure her?"

With this the man leapt to his feet, waved his hands in the air, and spurted out, "I said, 'I do' fifty years ago, not 'I don't!'"

Men, Scripture admonishes us to "love our wives as Christ loved the church." What does that mean? It means that men are to follow Christ's model of initiating. Christ took the initiative in forgiveness, so must the husband. The man needs to apologize first. That is biblical. Christ is patient with us, wanting none of us to perish. Likewise, husbands, be patient with your wives. They are tender and are to be treasured. Christ loved us while we were still sinners. He did not wait for us to love Him back. Guys, are you seeing the pattern here? We are to be loving to our wives, not just when we say, "I do" like the cold-hearted grump from our story.

In four places in the New Testament, the husband is commanded to love his wife. Not once does it mention that the wife is to love her husband. Do you think it is because we are hard-headed or hard-hearted? Neither one will make your marriage flourish.

Pray for God to increase your intentionality with each other. Men, ask the Lord to heighten your awareness of how to lead in love.

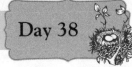

*Husbands, love your wives, just as Christ also
loved the church and gave Himself up for her.*
Ephesians 5:25

I had a friend who owned his own business. Friends were always complimenting him on his accomplishments and asking what it was like to be his own boss. One of his favorite sayings was, "Well, I am the CEO and COJ – Chief Operating Janitor!"

He makes a good point. Leadership comes with responsibility and humility. Men, in leading your family, you must humble yourself. The leader sets the tone for the rest of the company, and so it is with husbands and the home.

Husbands are to initiate action and set a tone of harmony in the home. So many men come home huffing and puffing. A tone is set. Instead of a loving and warm environment, wives and kids often feel like they are walking on eggshells. This is against God's command for the home. He says men are to love their wives as Christ loved the Church – patiently, whole-heartedly, freely, sacrificially, and forgivingly.

Men, I challenge you to be the CEO and the COL– Chief Operating Lover of your home!

Pray for God to increase your ability to set a harmonious and loving tone in your home. Men, ask that the Lord lovingly show you how He loves first!

In this same way, husbands ought to love their wives as their own bodies. He who loves his wife loves himself. After all, no one ever hated their own body, but they feed and care for their body, just as Christ does the church – for we are members of His body. **Ephesians 5:28-30 NIV**

I s your home a happy place? Often home is viewed as the place to sleep, but not a true desirable destination. There is no laughter, no joy, no feeling. Often when we see this scenario, the emotions have gone because the husband has not loved his wife as Christ loves the Church. Men, we are to love our wives as we love our own bodies. We don't pick out a deformity in our own body and call attention to it all the time. Quite the opposite. Psychologists say we compensate for any shortcomings we feel we have. *Compensate* is just a fancy way of saying we build up other areas. You've seen the little guy who becomes a muscle-bound body-builder.

It is the same with your wife. Too many times, I have heard a man say, "Well, let me tell you what my crazy wife did." He would then proceed to tell a story that was demeaning and embarrassing to her. Are you building her up or tearing her down?

As you strengthen your love for your wife, you will be strengthening your marriage and your home. My bet is joy, laughter, and emotion will return to your home, and it will be a much sought-after destination for your entire family!

Pray for God to increase your ability to set a harmonious and loving tone in your home and to help you build up, rather than tear down.

In this same way, husbands ought to love their wives as their own bodies. He who loves his wife loves himself. After all, no one ever hated their own body, but they feed and care for their body, just as Christ does the church – for we are members of His body. **Ephesians 5:28-30 NIV**

A commercial for a vacation destination showed film footage of happy people in beautiful surroundings. The announcer said, "Enjoy the warm, welcoming hospitality of our people. Come relax, unwind, and enjoy. Once you experience it, you'll want to return over and over again." I could not help but think to myself, "That is what I want my home to be!"

Jo Beth has made our home a destination. Whenever I travel or have to be away for any period of time, my heart longs to return home. Home is where she most desires to be as well. Our home fits the ad. It is warm with welcoming hospitality. She serves me, and I serve her. We work at making sure we demonstrate "hospitality" to each other. It is a place we can relax, unwind, and enjoy. We have fun there.

Parents and spouses, it is vitally important to make your home not only a haven of warmth and security, but a fun place to be.

Biblically, it is my responsibility to set the tone of love and warmth in our home. I know most people think it is the wife's. She is responsible for certain aspects. But do not miss the fact that the man's responsibility is to set the tone. If I am loving my wife as I love my own body – making sure she is fed physically and spiritually, rested, secure, cherished and cared for – then the right tone will be set. A beautiful and enjoyable destination will be established, a place worth returning to over and over again!

Pray for God to help you establish a warm and welcoming destination in your home. Men, ask that the Lord lovingly show you how to love your wife as you do your own body.

Then Jesus again spoke to them, saying, "I am the Light of the world; he who follows Me will not walk in the darkness, but will have the Light of life."
John 8:12

Yesterday, I told you about an inspiring commercial advertising a vacation destination. I described the opening words about hospitality and the visual of happy people frolicking in the sun. At the very end of the commercial, additional words got me to thinking again about the impact of establishing an inviting destination for your family at home. The announcer returns to say with dramatic emphasis, "To truly experience the light that is our destination, you must experience it for yourself. It emanates from our hearts. It is visible everywhere. It changes everything it touches. It will change you. The light of the Caribbean is calling."

Again it struck me. Our home is light-filled. I don't mean we have a lamp on in every room. I mean it is Christ-centered and emanates the true Light of the World. Our sons have grown and left our house, but I still run into their childhood friends every now and then. Often, one will bring up a funny story about hanging out at our house when they were young. Every now and then, someone will say that they enjoyed being there because it was so different from the strife-filled home in which they lived.

This breaks my heart.

We do not have the perfect family or the perfect home, but what we do have is The Light. It emanates from our hearts and is visible everywhere. It changes everything it touches, and it will change you. The light that is calling is Jesus. Is He the light in your home?

Pray for Jesus to be the light emanating from your heart and your home. Invite Him in and see how much your home will change.

*Be kind to one another, tender-hearted, forgiving each
other, just as God in Christ also has forgiven you.*
Ephesians 4:32

D o you want the secret to a Happy Home? Then you need to follow one
verse: *"Be kind to one another, tender-hearted, forgiving each other, just
as God in Christ also has forgiven you."* This one command is the single most
important verse regarding marriage and the home.

I knew a godly man who had been married over fifty years, which at the time
seemed like an eternity to me. The interesting thing was the joy, exuberance,
and sweet flirtation I always observed in his marriage. I have never forgotten
something he practiced. Each morning, he rose very early to go to work. He
would fix the coffee pot and leave a china cup out for his wife, as opposed to his
old mug. However, the thing that really stuck with me is that he would leave a
little love note underneath her cup and saucer. He would tear a piece of paper
towel, a part of an envelope, a newspaper coupon, or whatever was handy and
jot a few loving words down for her eyes only.

Her first encounter every morning was a love note. Nothing poetic, simply
short, sweet, and true words! "You are my sweetheart." "I love you." "You are
beautiful." "Have a great day, Love." "It's rainy today, but you are my sunshine!"
And so it went. Little thoughts, little gestures…HUGE results.

Do you want your marriage to sizzle and to last? Be kind, tenderhearted,
and forgiving.

*Ask the Lord for His creativity in being kind, tenderhearted, and romantic to each
other, and pray for an attitude of forgiveness, as you have been forgiven.*

A gentle answer turns away wrath, but a harsh word stirs up anger.
Proverbs 15:1

Nobel Peace Prize nominee Carl Rogers was a leading psychologist of the twentieth century. He is known for his therapeutic technique called *unconditional positive regard*. Basically, he believed that individuals come into a counseling office with all kinds of emotional and spiritual hurts. The one thing each and every person needs is for someone to give total empathy – or *unconditional positive regard*.

I believe this is a wonderful tool for marriage. Your spouse is the one person who should offer you unconditional openness and positive and authentic empathy. Empathy is a word that is often confused with sympathy. However, the term is very different from having pity on someone. Empathy is the ability to come alongside another in a certain situation as if it were your own. Webster's Dictionary defines empathy as "vicarious experiencing of the feelings, thoughts, or attitudes of another."

Jo Beth demonstrates this in our marriage and in our family. She comes alongside me and takes on my issues as her own. When I have been hurt, she hurts. When I have a success, she is ecstatic. When I need to vent, she is the ear that I seek, hands down! Over the years, we have grown into each other's best counselor. Second only to the Lord, it is her gentle answer and gentle listening I seek most.

By the way, Carl Rogers was not nominated for the Nobel Peace Prize in psychology. Instead, his nomination was for his efforts to bring peace to the peoples of South Africa and Northern Ireland. His theory, much like our scripture today, was one of peace.

Ask God, through His Holy Spirit to give you unconditional positive regard for your spouse.

Husbands, love your wives, just as Christ also loved the church and gave Himself up for her, so that He might sanctify her, having cleansed her by the washing of water with the Word, that He might present to Himself the church in all her glory, having no spot or wrinkle or any such thing; but that she would be holy and blameless.
Ephesians 5:25-31

Husbands, love your wives. If I were sending an old fashioned telegram, this is where I would say, "Stop." You do not have to be a Bible scholar to get this. It is all about L-O-V-E. Husbands, that is your job.

Now here is where it gets tricky. In the Greek, the verb love is in present tense, which means it is a continuous action. Before I lose you guys, let me translate: You have to keep showing her love. Christ came into this world with intention and purpose – to show us His love. He came to sacrifice. His actions and His words demonstrated His sacrificial love. You must be intentional and you must be purposeful or YOU WILL MISS THE MARK.

Scripture gives us the example, because dealing with the opposite sex can be tricky. We are created differently. Therefore, if a man follows the Apostle Paul's example, "Love your wives as Christ loved the Church and gave Himself up for her," he will be connecting with her on the right level.

Go for it guys, and be prepared to be amazed!

Pray today for intentional and purposeful demonstrations of love in your marriage.

Husbands, love your wives, just as Christ also loved the church and gave Himself up for her, so that He might sanctify her, having cleansed her by the washing of water with the Word, that He might present to Himself the church in all her glory, having no spot or wrinkle or any such thing; but that she would be holy and blameless.
Ephesians 5:25-31

God modeled human marriage after the relationship Christ has with us. Marriage is an illustration of the way God loves us—being totally committed to us, forgiving us, making us holy, spotless, and righteous through His sacrifice.

On the wedding day, the bride and the groom look as radiant and perfect as they ever will. The groom is perfectly attired and awaits his bride's entrance with great hope and great desire. The bride is flawlessly coiffed. She shines with adoration and expectancy. She is even becoming a different legal entity: her name will change.

However, after the name change and after the honeymoon, the couple will not appear as flawless to one another. So how can two imperfect people maintain the radiance? The Apostle Paul tells us how. The husband must cleanse his bride with the washing of the Word, so she can maintain the holy and blameless position of her wedding day. It is only through the Word of God that we enrich our understanding of God. As the husband and wife read the Bible together, the transforming power of the Holy Spirit will increase the Christ-likeness in both people. As each reflects Christ to the other, the radiance and beauty of Jesus will shine through, and the commitment, forgiveness, holiness, and righteousness will inspire many, many more honeymoons.

Pray for the intentional washing of the Word together and extended honeymoons inspired by sacrificial love for each other.

"May he kiss me with the kisses of his mouth! For your love is better than wine. Your oils have a pleasing fragrance, and your name is like purified oil. Therefore, the maidens love you. Draw me after you and let us run together! The king has brought me into his chambers." **Song of Solomon 1:2-4**

Sex can just be sex, or it can be a thousand times better when based on emotional and spiritual intimacy. Spiritual intimacy is a divine mystery. But just as emotional intimacy takes work, so does physical intimacy. I read a funny quote by a small child who said, "King Solomon had 700 wives and 300 porcupines."

Well, I imagine with that many women all needing one man, they may have felt like porcupines. But aside from Solomon's disobedience to God in taking on foreign wives, he wrote a book that the Holy Spirit inspired. It is a love song. Within this tome, he is very specific on how to become a good lover to his wife.

His wife also writes about how to make love to her husband. Many of you are reading this thinking, "I can't believe this is in the Bible." Well, read it for yourself. It is all in there. Part of what you will find is a romance that is gentle, sweet, respectful, and sensual.

Here is an exercise for you. Take the next few days and read Song of Solomon to each other. Men, you read the king's part.(Ladies, this is how I get him to participate.) Ladies, read the part of the wife.

Remember, when Solomon was made king, God asked him how He could bless him. Solomon asked for wisdom. Within this book you will find wisdom for a loving and fulfilling marriage bed.

Ask God for emotional, spiritual, and physical intimacy in your marriage.

Put on then as God's chosen ones, holy and beloved, compassionate hearts, kindness, humility, meekness, and patience, bearing with one another and, if one has a complaint against another, forgiving each other; as the Lord has forgiven you, so you also must forgive. Above all these, put on love, which binds everything together in perfect harmony. **Colossians 3:12-14**

Today's scripture perfectly describes a Happy Home. Is there a place you can go that has compassionate hearts, kindness, humility, meekness, and patience emanating from the people within? What about when you do have a complaint against each other? Is it handled quickly and forgiven?

Picture a house. You are on the outside. It is faded and no lights are on inside. Now imagine as you read these verses, that with each attribute described, a light begins to glow from within. A compassionate heart turns the light on. From behind the curtains, the house begins to glow. Next, the kindness light comes on and the inside glow becomes brighter. Humility notches up the brightness even more. Now the house looks warm and inviting.

From across the street, you notice that meekness turns on the front porch lanterns. Patience kicks on the landscape lighting, and you notice that the house does not seem as faded, but instead, bright and inviting. Last you see silhouetted through the curtains, a couple embrace…arms extended to enfold two small children. That is the love that binds that faded old house in perfect harmony.

Is this a picture of your home?

Today, ask the Lord to guide and light your path in establishing a Colossians 3 home.

Beloved, let us love one another, for love is from God; and everyone who loves is born of God and knows God.
I John 4:7

Do you know your partner's love language? When I was courting Jo Beth prior to our marriage, we did not know the term, "love language." I wish we had; but I could begin to see what outward expressions of love worked with her, and she began to understand how I received love. In his widely read book, *The Five Love Languages,* Dr. Gary Chapman has deciphered the language of love into these categories. They are:

1. Words of Affirmation

2. Quality Time

3. Receiving Gifts

4. Acts of Service

5. Physical Touch

Make it a point to find out what language your mate is speaking. Many times I see couples who are struggling in their marriage because they do not know how to interpret their partner's love language. This language is easy to learn once you investigate it with your spouse. As an exercise today, ask your mate which of the five love languages speaks most clearly to him/her. Then begin to practice, practice, practice your spouse's native love language. If you already know it, don't forget that practice helps you become fluent!

Pray for the Lord to guide you in deciphering your partner's love language. Ask for the Lord to help interpret and guide you in expressing love to your spouse in a language other than your own.

Beloved, let us love one another, for love is from God; and everyone who loves is born of God and knows God. **I John 4:7**

A woman asked her husband, "What makes you feel loved?"

After several moments passed, he said, "Sunflower seeds."

"Sunflower seeds?" repeated the wife.

"Yep. I like sunflower seeds."

"Okaaaaaaay," she replied confused.

He laughed and shared the reason, "When I was a kid and my parents were going through a bitter divorce, I hung out with my grandfather a lot. One day I was running errands with him to stay away from my parents' house. He was checking out at a register of the hardware store, and he handed me a bag of sunflower seeds. Surprised, I asked, 'What are these for?' He said, 'Cause you're a really good grandson.' I never forgot it."

The woman smiled. After that, she made it a priority to leave packages of sunflower seeds for him in unexpected places.

She learned how to speak the love language of sunflower seeds.

What is your mate's sunflower seed?

Pray for the Lord to guide you in learning how to communicate love to your partner.

And do not get drunk with wine, for that is dissipation, but be filled with the Spirit, speaking to one another in psalms and hymns and spiritual songs, singing and making melody with your heart to the Lord; always giving thanks for all things in the name of our Lord Jesus Christ to God, even the Father; and be subject to one another in the fear of Christ. Wives, be subject to your own husbands, as to the Lord. For the husband is the head of the wife, as Christ also is the head of the church, He Himself being the Savior of the body. But as the church is subject to Christ, so also the wives ought to be to their husbands in everything. Husbands, love your wives, just as Christ also loved the church and gave Himself up for her, so that He might sanctify her, having cleansed her by the washing of water with the word, that He might present to Himself the church in all her glory, having no spot or wrinkle or any such thing; but that she would be holy and blameless. So husbands ought also to love their own wives as their own bodies. He who loves his own wife loves himself; for no one ever hated his own flesh, but nourishes and cherishes it, just as Christ also does the church, because we are members of His body. For this reason a man shall leave his father and mother and shall be joined to his wife, and the two shall become one flesh. This mystery is great; but I am speaking with reference to Christ and the church. Nevertheless, each individual among you also is to love his own wife even as himself, and the wife must see to it that she respects her husband. **Ephesians 5:18-33**

The Bible gives us a map for marriage. Instructions are crystal clear. If you want your marriage to be fulfilling and successful, this is the way to go. Just having a map does not necessarily point us in the right direction. We need a compass to show us north, south, east, and west. Webster's dictionary defines Cardinal Points, as "the four principal directional compass points north, south, east, and west." So I want to provide a compass to help us find the Cardinal Points for marriage.

North on the marriage map is submission – the principle of marriage. South is covenant – the definition of marriage. West is oneness, or intimacy –the goal of marriage. East on the marriage map is friendship – the purpose of marriage.

As we navigate this map together, we will refer to these Cardinal Points on our compass. We will explore in each direction, and uncover the bountiful richness of God's plan for marriage.

Pray that the Holy Spirit will be your ultimate compass, giving direction and guidance to your marriage. Ask today for a sharpened ability to live out Ephesians 5 in your home.

…and be subject to one another in the fear of Christ. **Ephesians 5:21**

As early as 1540, true north, true south, true east, and true west were referred to as the Cardinal Points. Within this context, Cardinal Point North on the Happy Home compass is submission. Ephesians 5:21 says that we are to be submissive *one to another.* This is the genius and the secret to any relationship. It reflects total respect. For a marriage, this is the operational principle and direction that will keep it steadily moving forward. A husband is to be submissive to his wife, and the wife to her husband. Remember, this is a prerequisite to all successful relationships. Paul lists the relationships: marriage, family, and the marketplace.

Years ago, a friend told me a story about playing a game of doubles tennis against two women from Japan. She describes how difficult it was to beat the Japanese women. She says the two women were so elegant, kind, and gracious that competition seemed meaningless. She describes the encounter like this:

> Each Japanese woman, dressed from head-to-toe in white, entered the court and bowed to us, then turned and faced each other to bow. Learning our names, each woman made sure that she could pronounce it. This would come in handy because every time they hit a shot, they actually announced where it was going, "Coming to you, Cathy, etc." After each opposing shot, the Japanese women called out encouragement, "Nice shot, Cathy," "Good try, Beth," "Worthy effort," or "Thank you for the point," etc.

My friends got a terrible case of the giggles. They had never seen true submission in action. This peculiar behavior was so inspiring they began to respond in kind. They began to see the game from the other team's point of view. When an opponent made a point, they felt pleased for her. When she hit it into the net, my friend says she actually felt a surge of compassion.

Today, my friend does not remember who won. Many tennis matches and many decades later, she remembers this one the most – not for the win or the loss, but for the most enjoyable match of her life. Score: Love all.

Pray that the Holy Spirit will be your ultimate compass, giving direction and guidance to your marriage. Ask to be empowered to submit, one to another, to facilitate graciousness and tenderheartedness in your home.

... and be subject to one another in the fear of Christ. Wives, be subject to your own husbands, as to the Lord. For the husband is the head of the wife, as Christ also is the head of the church, He Himself being the Savior of the body. But as the church is subject to Christ, so also the wives ought to be to their husbands in everything.
Ephesians 5:21-24

As we learned yesterday, Cardinal Point North on the Happy Home compass is submission. Ephesians 5:21 says that we are to be submissive one to another, and this is the true north. But the passage continues and becomes even more specific in terms of the marriage compass. As we model ourselves after Jesus Christ, we move from our natural in-born state of selfishness to being servants, but it is through the Holy Spirit that we become submissive.

Our passage says we are to be subject to one another. This is literally a military word. We are "to salute." We are to position ourselves under one another. However, the role the Bible describes for the woman is one of empowerment. She is to be a helpmate. A helper is someone who empowers others. Women do that better than men. Therefore, she is not stripped of her power, but instead takes her unique power and supports her husband with it.

General Omar Bradley was a venerable field commander who led our US troops in the invasion of Normandy and many other strategic feats in World War II. He ultimately commanded forty-three divisions and 1.3 million men. After the war, he made this statement about the success and the support of military submission: "The greatness of a leader is measured by the achievements of the led."

Husbands, recognize your wife has resources you do not have. Likewise, men bring something to the marriage that the woman cannot bring. In God's design, marriage is a voluntary empowering of one equal to another equal – each bringing different assets, abilities, and roles.

Pray the Holy Spirit will empower you to submit one to another. Wives, ask for the ability to empower your husband through submission. Husbands, ask for godly leadership and submission to the ultimate authority of Christ Jesus.

… and be subject to one another in the fear of Christ. Wives, be subject to your own husbands, as to the Lord. For the husband is the head of the wife, as Christ also is the head of the church, He Himself being the Savior of the body. But as the church is subject to Christ, so also the wives ought to be to their husbands in everything.

Ephesians 5:21-24

This passage may be one of the most abused scriptures in the Bible. It has been brandished like a weapon by men. Even non-believing men seem to know this command. Often, the harsh or the arrogant use this scripture against their wives instead of for their wives.

Similarly, women have reviled this passage as something intended to be severe or controlling – written by a man for a man.

Both are inaccurate. We must remember that this is the application of the Cardinal Point North: submission. The principle of submission is the general category and applies to both parties in the relationship. In the case of Christian husbands and wives, it is to be done by both. Only the methods of subjection will differ according to the sex, but the principle remains the same.

Paul gets specific on what this means for each gender. He explains how the wife submits to her husband and how he submits to his wife, both out of reverence to Christ. The Greek word used for submission means, "adapt yourself to the authority of, or will of another; to arrange one's self under." This is the fulfillment of God's original design in the first marriage: Adam and Eve. God said she was to be "a helpmate for man." (Gen 2:20)

The apostle immediately clarifies the reason for submission: "as to the Lord." This tells us that her primary relationship is with the Lord. She is not yielding to her husband because he is wonderful (though I pray, ladies that your husband is). She is yielding to him because the Lord is wonderful, and it is pleasing to Him that she walk in her God-given position as a helper to her husband.

Therefore, in the context of this sacred submission, the voluntary surrender of our rights and self-interest is for the benefit of others and for the glory of God.

Pray for sacred submission. Pray together asking for guidance for wives to submit to their husbands "as unto Him," and for the husbands to have reverence and true enlightenment for this scripture.

... and be subject to one another in the fear of Christ. Wives, be subject to your own husbands, as to the Lord. For the husband is the head of the wife, as Christ also is the head of the church, He Himself being the Savior of the body. But as the church is subject to Christ, so also the wives ought to be to their husbands in everything.
Ephesians 5:21-24

Going back to the beginning of creation helps enlighten us as to God's intent for marital roles. Genesis 2:18 says, "The Lord God said, 'It is not good for man to be alone, so I will make a helper for him.'" So God's original idea was that the wife, the woman, would be the helper. Many women have decried that title. They often express indignation at being considered the side-kick, or the assistant.

Let me clarify this. In the original language, the word that is used here for helper is also used later in the Bible to describe the Lord. This word describes God as *our helper* and *our shield*, and *our helper and our strength*, and *our helper and our refuge*. Is it a slight or a put-down to describe God this way? Of course not!

Therefore, remember that the helper "arranges himself underneath" someone else to provide a benefit to that person. God comes underneath us to lift us above our circumstances with His power and protection. The wife arranges herself under her husband to use her power to help him in areas he is lacking.

Women, know with confidence that you are asked to submit as a helper, the very word used to describe God's characteristics, because you are in possession of unique attributes that your "Adam" was created without.

Wives, pray to be a helpmate to your husband. Ask the Lord to increase your awareness that He is your helper.

... and be subject to one another in the fear of Christ. Wives, be subject to your own husbands, as to the Lord. For the husband is the head of the wife, as Christ also is the head of the church, He Himself being the Savior of the body. But as the church is subject to Christ, so also the wives ought to be to their husbands in everything.
Ephesians 5:21-24

There is a sacred submission between a husband and wife. Though the roles are different, the balance should be equal. Paul describes this holy balance in a way that makes me think of a stage play. Both husbands and wives have a part. Husbands have the auspicious privilege of portraying the headship of Christ over the Church. In this role as husband, the man acts out sacrificial leadership, loving and fully submitting to God the Father.

Wives have the privilege to symbolically represent the Church in its submission to Jesus Christ. She does this by willingly adapting to the will of another: Christ, who is represented by her husband. In these divinely appointed roles, marriage takes on new symbolism. It is not merely two people attracted to each other who think they may want to hang out together for the rest of their lives. No! It is so much more.

Marriage is the ultimate symbol of Christ and the Church. This blessed balance, this holy matrimony should be reflected in the attitude and behavior of both husband and wife…sacred submission.

Pray for sacred submission and for a keen awareness of your role in this holiest of unions.

... and be subject to one another in the fear of Christ. Wives, be subject to your own husbands, as to the Lord. For the husband is the head of the wife, as Christ also is the head of the church, He Himself being the Savior of the body. But as the church is subject to Christ, so also the wives ought to be to their husbands in everything.
Ephesians 5:21-24

When my boys were younger, we loved to play basketball together. I possessed an understanding of the game they did not have. I had different skills and a higher aptitude in some areas of basketball. I spent many joyful hours teaching each boy how to dribble, pass, shoot, and jump. You see, since I knew more about the game, I could help each son with his game. I could use that power to bring myself under him, enable him, and advance him to places where he could not go by himself.

As crazy as it sounds, this is an example of femininity. It really is! This is what Scripture is referring to when it says that the helper is to be subject to her husband. She is to come up under him and use her feminine characteristics – which are different than those of her husband – to help him improve and succeed.

I hope that both male and female will see that when this biblical direction is followed, both become better players, and both are on the same winning team!

Pray for a team approach to your marriage.

... and be subject to one another in the fear of Christ. Wives, be subject to your own husbands, as to the Lord. For the husband is the head of the wife, as Christ also is the head of the church, He Himself being the Savior of the body. But as the church is subject to Christ, so also the wives ought to be to their husbands in everything.
Ephesians 5:21-24

I once saw something that was hauntingly sad: the head of a doll, with its body long ago separated and lost, among other abandoned toys and childhood memories. Digging through the rummage, I secretly hoped to find the body and to restore the doll to her original state and in some ways her imaginary dignity.

Much later, as I was studying Ephesians 5, the doll popped into my mind. The head needs a body, just as the body needs the head. Often we focus on the head: the husband. He represents Christ as head of the Church. Certainly, in a human, the head directs the body on how to operate and function. The body is under the authority of the head.

The little doll head reminded me of the importance of the body and how disconnected the head is without it. The head, the husband, has nothing to lead without the body – no arms, no legs, no hands or feet. These are the parts of the body that help. Under the direction of the head, the hands feed, they nurture, and they reach out to others. The feet walk and carry on even when weary.

I am sure the doll must have been a treasure at one time, but at that time, the head and the body must have been in perfect union.

Prayerfully consider the treasure that the union of the head and body form in holy matrimony.

Children, obey your parents in the Lord, for this is right. Honor your father and mother, which is the first commandment with a promise, so that it may be well with you, and that you may live long on the earth. Fathers, do not provoke your children to anger, but bring them up in the discipline and instruction of the Lord.

Ephesians 6:1-4

Submission is the due North Cardinal Point, which gives all relationships direction. However, "honor" implies a voluntary act of respect. Many people do not have parents who have earned earthly respect from their children. Counseling offices and prisons are full of the evidence of the destructive influence parents can have on children. Perhaps this is why our Heavenly Father gives us a promise – like a sweet reward – if we follow His command to obey and to honor our parents. He says that if we submit to this commandment, it will be well with us, and we will have a full life on earth.

Recently, a lovely woman sat across from me, wrestling with a major life decision: reconciliation with her alcoholic mother who had abused her verbally and physically and kicked her out of the house when she was just 16 years old. She had struggled to stay in class and finish high school. Through sheer determination and sleepless nights, she studied and worked hard and became a medical professional. Now decades later, she was seeking counsel.

Her estranged mother, now broke and alone, lived 400 miles away. Though her mother had three children, the other two had forged lives for themselves that did not include the raging and abusive mother of their past. The older woman's health was not good as a result of the years of addiction, and our church member was making arrangements to bring her mother to live with her. I asked her how she felt about her mother now. She replied that she had forgiven her.

"That's good," I continued, "Yet, you are doing more than forgiving…you are bringing the woman who kicked you out at 16 years of age to live with you."

Tears rolled down her cheeks as she said, "She has no one."

I replied, "She has someone very special. She has you."

This is what it means to honor your parents. Long ago, a line had been drawn in the sand. Different life paths emerged, but the biblical direction of submission brought this mother and child back together.

Pray for God to increase your awareness of ways to honor your parents, and pray that you will be a parent who does not provoke, but instead, leads through submission to the Lord.

Children, obey your parents in the Lord, for this is right. Honor your father and mother, which is the first commandment with a promise, so that it may be well with you, and that you may live long on the earth. Fathers, do not provoke your children to anger, but bring them up in the discipline and instruction of the Lord.

Ephesians 6:1-4

Fathers are instructed not to provoke their children to anger, but to *"bring them up in the discipline and instruction of the Lord."* This is an interesting passage because the last part is the most significant: *in the discipline and instruction of the Lord.* Parents, the only way that you can accomplish this is to be totally submitted to the Lord yourself.

I saw this personally demonstrated one harrowing evening at a hospital many years ago. Tropical Storm Allison was beating Houston to a pulp and we were enveloped in darkness and torrential rain day and night. A church member was at the hospital with her beloved father. He was a heart patient and dependent on electronic medical devices to keep him alive. The medical center was flooded and experiencing power outages.

A few of us had volunteered to bring a chest full of ice and cold drinks to our friend and her family. When we got there, the elevator was out, so we entered the dimly lit stairwell and carried the heavy cooler up eleven flights of stairs. Breathless and sweating profusely, we entered the eleventh floor to see total chaos. The hospital was largely operating on back-up generators located in the basement, which was flooding even as we climbed the stairs. Life-giving machines were blinking off, and doctors and nurses were scrambling to give manual life-support to many people.

We saw our friend who was tending to the needs of her sick father. As we approached her, she was calm and serene. Her father lived through it, praise God.

Later she told us that amid the cacophony of fearful voices, anguished moans, shouted instructions and frantic pleas, her sweet father's voice floated up to her. Through his pain, though in and out of lucidity, he sang hymns and quoted Scripture. She said something that has always stuck with me, "When illness presses in, you never know what will come out. For Dad, what came out was his faith in God."

What a portrait of a father surrendered to his Heavenly Father and a daughter, honoring her father even through the storm.

As parents, pray to be fully submitted to your own Heavenly Father. As a child, pray for a spirit of honor and respect toward your earthly parents.

Children, obey your parents in the Lord, for this is right. Honor your father and mother, which is the first commandment with a promise, so that it may be well with you, and that you may live long on the earth. Fathers, do not provoke your children to anger, but bring them up in the discipline and instruction of the Lord.

Ephesians 6:1-4

I remember a particularly rowdy family road trip. I would call it a vacation, but driving anywhere with the entire family cramped in the car for hours upon hours is more of a trip than a vacation. In those days, we did not have fancy SUVs where everyone had their own entertainment monitors, headsets, and drink holders. We did not even know where all of the seatbelts were!

So it was in this setting that my wife became exasperated with the boisterous bunch and quipped, "Children, obey your parents, because the Lord says it's right!"

From somewhere in the far back seat, we heard the voice of the youngest rabble-rouser pipe in, "Father, do not provoke your children to anger!"

We looked at each other, speechless. I finished the verse, "Well honey, I guess we brought them up in the instruction of the Lord, or he wouldn't have known that verse."

Pray for joyful times together, and memory-making moments.

Slaves, be obedient to those who are your masters according to the flesh, with fear and trembling, in the sincerity of your heart, as to Christ; not by way of eye service, as men-pleasers, but as slaves of Christ, doing the will of God from the heart. With good will render service, as to the Lord, and not to men, knowing that whatever good thing each one does, this he will receive back from the Lord, whether slave or free.

Ephesians 6:5-8

We continue in our look at submission. A Happy Home is comprised of many relationships. One aspect is that those in the home have a purpose and a calling. Many people love their jobs and their co-workers. They get up every day ready to tackle their work. Other people live to retire. They hate their jobs, dislike their bosses, and work merely to have money to live. God has something to say about this.

Our scripture today refers to slaves and masters, or in today's context, employees and employers. Paul is encouraging each of us to perform our vocations with excellence. We are to work as if God is our boss, which He ultimately is.

In the 1950s, a famous psychological experiment was performed in a factory. The workers were told that new lighting was being considered, so they would be observed in both lights to see which lighting increased productivity.

The productivity almost doubled. However, no lighting was altered. The experiment proved that because the workers thought they were being observed, they performed with excellence.

With so much of our time spent working, it is imperative that we do not let an unhappy work attitude affect our family. Happy Homes have workers who have submitted their work to the Lord.

Pray for a renewal of dedication to your work. Ask that God would enable you to perform with excellence in all things, for His glory.

And masters, do the same things to them, and give up threatening, knowing that both their Master and yours is in Heaven, and there is no partiality with Him.
Ephesians 6:9

As we look at submission in all areas of relationships and how it affects the home, the boss-employee relationship comes to light. Ross Perot is a controversial political figure. However, with thousands of employees, his success as a businessman is undisputed. He is ranked by Forbes as the 101st-richest person in the United States, with an estimated net worth of about $3.5 billion in 2012.

This is what he says about how to treat the people who work for you:

> *"Never ask anyone to do what you haven't done before and wouldn't do again. That's a pretty fundamental rule in leadership...treat them like you treat yourself. Things you don't like, they don't like. You don't like to be jerked around - they don't either. You don't like to be talked down to, and they don't either. You would rather work with somebody than for somebody. So would they. You hate people who pound on your head after you gave everything you had and failed... It's that simple."*

It sounds to me like he has Ephesians 6:9 down pat. And for the record, that Forbes' ranking indicates he puts his money where his mouth is.

Pray to lead with a submissive spirit. Ask the Lord to remind you who the Master really is.

For this reason a man shall leave his father and mother and shall be joined to his wife, and the two shall become one flesh. This mystery is great; but I am speaking with reference to Christ and the church. Nevertheless, each individual among you also is to love his own wife even as himself, and the wife must see to it that she respects her husband. **Ephesians 5:31-33**

South on the Happy Home Compass is covenant. This is the very definition of marriage. A covenant is binding. The two separate people are bound to one another and to God. Consider the covenant God made with Abraham.

- God called Abraham to leave his home and family.

- Abraham was called to begin a journey, willing to go wherever God wanted him to go.

- A name change took place: Abram was named Abraham.

- God and Abraham exchanged something to signify the covenant. God gave Abraham land and Abraham was circumcised.

- The children received the inheritance.

Do you see the parallels to marriage? The Bible tells us that the man is called to leave his father and mother and to be joined with his wife. This begins the journey. Similarly, the couple is renamed. They become "Mr. and Mrs." and she takes on his legal name. Vows and rings are exchanged to symbolize the covenant. And finally, the children born to the couple have the inheritance of their parents' name, commitment to each other, and commitment to God.

The covenant is a sacred bonding between a man, a woman, and God.

❖◦•◦•◦————➤✦◦•◦•◦————❖

Pray to fully comprehend the sacred and holy union of your marriage covenant.

For this reason a man shall leave his father and mother and shall be joined to his wife, and the two shall become one flesh. This mystery is great; but I am speaking with reference to Christ and the church. Nevertheless, each individual among you also is to love his own wife even as himself, and the wife must see to it that she respects her husband. **Ephesians 5:31-33**

I n ancient times, a covenant was always entered with reverence. There was a covenant made between God and Abraham. When Abraham made the covenant with God, he cut animals in half and God passed between them to complete the covenant. In ancient wedding ceremonies, the bride's family and the groom's family would bring animals. They would cut them in half and place each half several feet apart. Then the bride and the groom would walk together through the "aisle" formed by the animals arranged on both sides. As they walked, the parents would say, "As God witnesses, may you die if this covenant is ever broken." This gives us great insight into how much the family wanted the couple to stay together.

Today, our wedding aisles are not formed by such a gruesome sight. Our wedding vows have also come down a notch: "'til death do us part." But the covenant is still one of great gravity. I am struck by the difference also in the participation of the family. I have performed many wedding ceremonies where I could barely get the couple alone because of the overbearing demands of the parents. *"For this reason,"* the Bible admonishes, *"a man shall leave his father and mother and shall be joined to his wife."*

At the altar, a covenant is cut. It is between the husband and wife.

Pray for a deeper understanding of your marriage covenant. Also ask for the ability to heed Ephesians 5.

Therefore shall a man leave his father and his mother, and shall cleave unto his wife: and they shall be one flesh. And they were both naked, the man and his wife, and were not ashamed. **Genesis 2:24 KJV**

As we continue to look at Cardinal Point South on the Happy Home compass, understanding the mystery of a covenant is crucial. Without a true south, our marriages would have no direction. Each Cardinal Point works like the points on a compass, giving balance and direction to the journey of marriage and family.

In current culture, covenant is rarely talked about. So let's examine the origins of the marriage covenant. Our scripture today uses the word, cleave. This word in Hebrew means "to cling onto, or to be attracted to as in metal to a magnet." The holy mystery of covenant is that through becoming one flesh, you actually become family. Just as each of us is born from our mother and father's union, we have their family genes. As close as that relationship is, the marriage covenant is closer. Scripture tells us that we are to leave the biological sameness that we have with our parents for the newly created spiritual sameness we now have with our spouse. Did you get that? You are now more closely related to your spouse than you are to your parents. This is the sacred mystery of holy matrimony.

Ask the Lord to impress upon you the sanctity of your covenant relationship with your spouse. Pray to understand more deeply the depth and the breadth of your oneness.

And do not get drunk with wine, for that is dissipation, but be filled with the Spirit, speaking to one another in psalms, and hymns, and spiritual songs, singing and making melody with your heart to the Lord; always giving thanks for all things in the name of our Lord Jesus Christ to God, even the Father; and be subject to one another in the fear of Christ. **Ephesians 5:18-21**

I magine with me, if you will, that you are sitting with about 5,000 people in our church sanctuary on a Sunday morning. Suddenly, an officer of the law comes through the door and says each one of us is going to board a military carrier bound for the deep sea. As we all file out and are taken to board the ship, the captain makes an announcement. "Only half of you will survive," he booms. The deep voice continues, "Half will be thrown overboard. Some will be rescued, but statistics show only half will return safely and triumphantly home." As you glance around, you see the name on the side of this great sea-going vessel is *MARRIAGE.*

I believe if you were on that carrier, and I stood up and said I wanted to give you some instructions about how you could be rescued if your ship hit a storm, you would listen! Ephesians 5 offers many of the safety instructions for the *MARRIAGE* vessel. Read it, meditate on it, and apply it to your marriage. God's desire is for each and every one of us to stay on board!

Pray that God will enlighten you through His Word, and that Ephesians 5 will become safety instructions that you refer to over and over again.

The man said, "This is now bone of my bones, and flesh of my flesh. She shall be called woman, because she was taken out of man." **Genesis 2:23**

Yesterday we talked about the safety, or rescue plan for marriage. Today I want to simplify the plan into three infallible components. Before you board the carrier **MARRIAGE**, these three safety rules must be in place. However, if you have already boarded, these easily convert into a rescue plan. For the next three days, we will look at each of these safety rules:

1. Friendship   2. Chemistry   3. Equal Yoke

Friendship. If you start out with friendship, you are saving your marriage before you get started. Remember, the purpose of marriage is friendship, or companionship. In God's very first design for marriage, He said, "It is not good for man to be alone." When Adam saw Eve, he said, "This is now bone of my bones, and flesh of my flesh...." What is he saying? He is saying, "Here, in your presence, I know who I am. I am whole." That is a reality. But a word of caution here: Remember, even though Adam was alone, he had a healthy, intimate relationship with God. When looking for your "Adam" or your "Eve", Christianity must be the first requisite.

Friendship is a close connection that creates a special bond. Friends are the people we want to be around. They can look into our lives, see our flaws, and like us anyway. If you are not married, look for a friend in your future spouse. If you are married, do everything possible to become best friends. Affirm each other. Laugh with each other. Spend time with each other. Accept each other. This is part of a safety plan that each of us needs.

Pray for a friend in your mate. Ask God, who calls us friends, to teach us how to be a friend to each other.

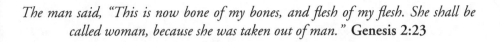
The man said, "This is now bone of my bones, and flesh of my flesh. She shall be called woman, because she was taken out of man." **Genesis 2:23**

Our *MARRIAGE* safety plan has three infallible components: friendship, chemistry, and equal yoke. Today, we will look at the second necessary element: chemistry.

Chemistry. The Greek word for this kind of love is *eros*. Eros is associated with sexual desire. Chemistry with your spouse is a crucial component. Many young people will take this as a "given." However, within the context of marriage, nothing can be taken for granted.

As our days fill up with the demands of life, we can often neglect to pay attention to something that is working well. However, the sexual intimacy between a husband and wife is a favorite target of the enemy. So we need to be on high alert to protect the chemistry in our marriage. Here are a few practical suggestions:

1. Pay attention to the physical part of your marriage. Make plans to be together. Anticipate times for a romantic interlude. Make it special.

2. Keep the bedroom sacred. Never argue in the bedroom, discipline children there, or pay bills there. The bedroom should be reserved for intimacy and sleeping between the couple. This will help you begin to associate your bedroom as a special place within your home.

3. Make it your goal to become the best possible lover to your mate. Two become one flesh. Pray that you will be spiritually one. Pray that your physical oneness will be all that God intends for it to be.

God will work through a lot of things in our marriage if we will put effort into understanding what it means to become one flesh. This is when your flesh and your marriage really begin to sizzle!

Pray for a godly understanding of becoming one. Ask God to help you become intentional and purposeful about keeping chemistry and sizzle active and alive in your marriage.

Do not be yoked together with unbelievers. For what do righteousness and wickedness have in common? Or what fellowship can light have with darkness? What harmony is there between Christ and Belial? Or what does a believer have in common with an unbeliever? **II Corinthians 6:14-15**

Our *MARRIAGE* safety plan has three infallible components: friendship, chemistry, and equal yoke. Today, we will look at the third necessary element: equal yoke.

Equal Yoke. Our scripture today uses an antiquated term, "yoke," which means *a coupling, as when two oxen are coupled, or yoked together by a pulling beam to do work such as plowing a field or pulling a wagon.* The term was very common during biblical times, as oxen were a primary means of providing farm work.

The phrase *"Do not be yoked together with unbelievers"* is the translation of just one Greek word, *heterozugeo*, which is a compound word meaning, *to yoke up differently; to associate discordantly; unequally yoke together.*

This should be the litmus test for both the friendship and the chemistry part of our safety plan. In the long run, it will be difficult to plow along together if you are completely different in your belief systems. Picture your friend and future mate being chained to you as oxen are. When he or she wants to turn and go down a path that does not align with your beliefs as a Christian, you are either going to get dragged along that dark path, or you will pull against each other.

Likewise, when you seek to become one-flesh with someone, you want to know that you are sharing a central and sacred belief in Jesus Christ. To become one-flesh with a non-believer is a dangerous position.

Test the safety equipment first: friendship and chemistry must pass the real test – are you tying yourself to someone who is tied to Jesus?

Pray to be equally yoked with someone who is yoked to Jesus Christ. Ask God to reveal the character and the beliefs of your potential partner.

For the rest of you who are in mixed marriages—Christian married to non-Christian—we have no explicit command from the Master. So this is what you must do. If you are a man with a wife who is not a believer but who still wants to live with you, hold on to her. If you are a woman with a husband who is not a believer but he wants to live with you, hold on to him. The unbelieving husband shares to an extent in the holiness of his wife, and the unbelieving wife is likewise touched by the holiness of her husband. **1 Corinthians 7: 12-14 MSG**

D o not forget that our *MARRIAGE* safety plan can also be a rescue plan if you are already married.

As we examine the third element of the plan, I want to address those of you who are already married to non-believers. I used The Message translation for today's scripture because it relates the idea in a clear, practical way: stay married. Once you have entered into a covenant, you must stay. In other words, you are on the *MARRIAGE* boat and are already out to sea – don't jump overboard!

Instead, treat your unbelieving spouse as if they were a Christian. Show them love and respect. Pray diligently for them. Allow God to pursue him or her in His timing. When children are involved, follow the biblical way of raising them. Look for all scriptures on parenting. The Bible offers instructions on "training up a child."

As you head out to sea on the *MARRIAGE* carrier, there will be storms. Helping your unbelieving spouse weather those storms with the wisdom and gentleness of the Holy Spirit may not just keep you married, but may save his or her soul.

Ask the Lord to change and open the heart of your unbelieving spouse. Ask for the patience and perseverance to stay onboard.

For this reason, a man shall leave his father and mother and shall be joined to his wife, and the two shall become one flesh. This mystery is great; but I am speaking with reference to Christ and the church. Nevertheless, each individual among you also is to love his own wife even as himself, and the wife must see to it that she respects her husband. **Ephesians 5:31-33**

West on the marriage compass is oneness. Perhaps the single greatest element of this wonderful mystery is when the Bible tells us that two people in marriage become one flesh. "One flesh" is a strong description. From it we can infer a possibility of deep unity and deep cohesion when two people of different genders enter into an intimate, public, permanent, enriching relationship. In this relationship of mutuality, two lives are shared with one another. This oneness is expressed both physically and spiritually.

When we get married we actually become a new compound in the spiritual aspect. Let me illustrate. We all know that oil and water do not mix. You can place them in the same container, shake it up, and they go right back to their separate elements. However, you can take sodium and mix it with chloride and you no longer have two separate elements: you have salt! The same principle applies to hydrogen and oxygen. When combined, these two distinctly different elements come together to become water. Therefore, these two different elements become one new substance. This is marital oneness.

Ask the Lord to bless your oneness and to give you a deep reverence for the new creation that was formed when you became one flesh.

For this reason, a man shall leave his father and mother and shall be joined to his wife, and the two shall become one flesh. This mystery is great; but I am speaking with reference to Christ and the church. Nevertheless, each individual among you also is to love his own wife even as himself, and the wife must see to it that she respects her husband. **Ephesians 5:31-33**

P art of the thrill of marriage is bringing the new spouse into the close family circle. However, there is always some danger involved in trying to incorporate each other into an already existing family unit. First, the covenant couple must establish themselves as a single unit – a new independent family. Leaving your parents does not mean that you will disregard or abandon them. You will, however, have a new priority: your spouse. Here are some practical suggestions of what it means to leave your father and mother.

1. **The husband-wife relationship is now the priority relationship.** All other relationships come after this one. Your relationship with your parents is now secondary. Women, this can be especially hard for a Daddy's girl. Be on guard against old habits that place you in a position where you rely on your father instead of your husband. Likewise, men, your mother is no longer the one to nurture you. Your wife is your helpmate. She is the primary woman in your life. You must become a "one-woman man."

2. **Leaving also means you will not tolerate any criticism about your mate from your parents.** Period. You have become one flesh. To criticize him or her is to criticize you!

3. **Leaving means your spouse's desires, opinions, suggestions and requests are more important than your parents'.**

4. **Leaving means you are to seek your spouse's support to meet your needs.** Your parents should no longer be your primary source of income, affection, safety, security, approval, or advice.

Implement these standards early in your marriage. If you have been married for a while, it is never too late to leave and cleave and to keep your covenant between you and God, not you and the rest of the family!

Ask the Lord to help you rightly adjust to your priority relationship. Pray for gentle but firm boundaries that protect your marriage from outside interference.

For this reason a man shall leave his father and his mother, and be joined to his wife; and they shall become one flesh. **Genesis 2:24**

The home is not simply a sociological unit based on a biological need. The home is not something that merely happened. The home - the family and marriage - were part of the mind of God and the plan of God. It is divine in nature and in origin. God planned it; God created it; and God established it. Marriage and family are not merely human things; they are divine, holy, and sacred.

In fact, the only direct word Jesus had about any sociological subject was about marriage and the family. He had clear words of instruction about the home and about relationships within the family – grandparents, parents, fathers, mothers, children, husbands, and wives. He taught about all of the intimacy that we find or should find within the home.

Does this give you a new perspective? Your home is divine, holy, and sacred. Be encouraged today that God is for you and your family. After all, it was part of His plan.

Ask the Lord to help you keep in mind the sacred nature of your home, marriage and family. Ask Him for a spiritual renewal within your family as you seek to serve Him and each other.

For this reason, a man shall leave his father and mother and shall be joined to his wife, and the two shall become one flesh. This mystery is great; but I am speaking with reference to Christ and the church. Nevertheless, each individual among you also is to love his own wife even as himself, and the wife must see to it that she respects her husband. **Ephesians 5:31-33**

There are three things that must be in place for you and your partner to become one flesh: joining, reprogramming, and performance. Today we will look at the first action, joining.

Joining. You join together and open your life to your mate. You say, "I have joined your team and you have joined mine." Within this team, you must share everything: the skills, the challenges, the faults, the failures, the wins, and the losses.

Joining means opening yourself up to your mate. You share your intimacies. You share your thoughts. Your mate has the same access to you as you do to your own body.

Many people fail on this point. They refuse to let the other person "in." We try to hide our flaws, our fears, and our secret thoughts. Unless you let your marriage partner have full access, true oneness cannot take place.

In marriage, we have to take the risk of being exposed. That is why God gives us the guidelines to help make each other a safe person with whom we can be vulnerable. He says that men are to love their wives as their own bodies. Similarly, women are commanded to respect their husbands. Between the two cushions of love and respect, there is a soft landing.

Ask the Lord to bless your oneness and to help you open up to each other. Pray for a deep and powerful access to each other's heart.

For this reason, a man shall leave his father and mother and shall be joined to his wife, and the two shall become one flesh. This mystery is great; but I am speaking with reference to Christ and the church. Nevertheless, each individual among you also is to love his own wife even as himself, and the wife must see to it that she respects her husband. **Ephesians 5:31-33**

I saw a fascinating program about conjoined twins. When the girls were born, their parents were told the babies would not make it through the night. Twenty-two years later these young ladies have not only survived, but thrived. The interesting thing is how different they are. One has curly hair and is more outgoing and vivacious. The other has straight, silky hair and is steady, calm, and dependable. Both girls are courageous and determined.

They share a body, but are two totally different people. Physically, one controls the left side, while her sister controls the right side of the body. Together they work in harmony. Defying even more odds, they worked to obtain a driver's license and to graduate from college. Each relies on the other's strengths and uniqueness to make their body and their life better. They are amazing.

I could not help but think about Ephesians 5 as I listened to the commentator share the story of the twins. Phrases like "one body, yet two separate people" rang in my ears. I believe this provides a beautiful illustration of marriage. Can you see the parallels?

I feel compelled to mention one last thing: they share one heart.

Pray for a deeper desire to explore the mysteries of your oneness with your spouse. Pray that your joining will strengthen one another.

For this reason, a man shall leave his father and mother and shall be joined to his wife, and the two shall become one flesh. This mystery is great; but I am speaking with reference to Christ and the church. Nevertheless, each individual among you also is to love his own wife even as himself, and the wife must see to it that she respects her husband. **Ephesians 5:31-33**

Many modern couples expect marriage to be the stuff of a Hollywood romance. They envision themselves holding hands with violins playing in the background; having a beautiful, dynamic sex life; enjoying romantic dinners; and leaving love notes strewn here and there –movie stuff. But hey! Don't touch my finances, and don't come between my friends and me!

Stop the film! Go to a commercial. This movie will not have a happy ending. Joining means coming together in everything. I realize this may not be a very contemporary approach, but marriage is not a contemporary invention. God designed it from the beginning.

Joining is a coming away from all else to enter into intimacy with another person in every aspect of life. Your mate is now your new best friend. Friends who do not make your mate comfortable are not your friends anymore, because you are now one flesh. If they reject or disrespect your spouse, they are doing it to you, too.

Similarly, some couples seem to think that their finances are more sacred and off limits than their own bodies. "You can have access to my body anytime you want," they reason, "but stay away from my bank account." This is foolishness. Becoming one, as we know, means you are a new compound, a new entity.

If you want to see a great romance, tune in to God's plan for marriage and become completely joined in all aspects with your own leading lady, or leading man.

Ask the Lord for a romance that is inclusive of each other and dependent on Him.

Husbands, go all out in your love for your wives, exactly as Christ did for the church—a love marked by giving, not getting. Christ's love makes the church whole. His words evoke her beauty. Everything he does and says is designed to bring the best out of her, dressing her in dazzling white silk, radiant with holiness. That is how husbands ought to love their wives. They're really doing themselves a favor—since they're already "one" in marriage. No one abuses his own body, does he? No. He feeds and pampers it. That's how Christ treats us, the church, since we are part of his body. This is why a man leaves father and mother and cherishes his wife. No longer two, they become "one flesh." This is a huge mystery, and I don't pretend to understand it all. What is clearest to me is the way Christ treats the church, and this provides a good picture of how each husband is to treat his wife, loving himself in loving her, and how each wife is to honor her husband. **Ephesians 5:25-33 MSG**

Joining has another principle attached: sanctification. This is a biblical word that usually gets bantered around in terms of marriage only after the wedding. You do not typically see this word on shower invitations, wedding websites, or gift registries. Poems and romantic love songs usually don't mention it either. Why?

Sanctification is a process that brings about purification. In fact, Webster's Dictionary defines sanctification this way, "to be set apart for a sacred purpose; purify." In the process of purification, something is always strained out. When you apply this to a person's life, we are usually talking about sin. Therefore, the method of straining or sifting out the dross can be painful.

Marriage is that process. The Bible gives guidelines to help make the process gentle and edifying, instead of harsh and abrupt. As a husband strives to help his wife become all she can be in Christ – "radiant, without stain, or wrinkle, or any other blemish" – the Bible tells him to love her sacrificially, giving himself up for her. He is to put all selfishness aside. For her to be holy, he must not lead her into sin, but work diligently to protect her from it. He is to speak gently to her, build her up, and protect her. As The Message so beautifully states, he *"loves himself in loving her!"*

Ask the Lord to bless your oneness and to give you a deep reverence for the new creation that was formed when you became one flesh.

For this reason, a man shall leave his father and mother and shall be joined to his wife, and the two shall become one flesh. This mystery is great; but I am speaking with reference to Christ and the church. Nevertheless, each individual among you also is to love his own wife even as himself, and the wife must see to it that she respects her husband. **Ephesians 5:31-33**

We defined three things that must be in place for you and your partner to become one flesh: joining, reprogramming, and performance. Today we will look at the second action, reprogramming.

From the moment of conception, our mothers have primary authority over programming us. For better or for worse, science has proved that the mother figure has tremendous influence on how we see ourselves, our level of self-worth, and our sense of security. This is all wrapped up in a theory called the Attachment Theory. Simply put, we develop as individuals according to the healthy or unhealthy level of attachment we have with a mother or caregiver. Children who have been given love, support, boundaries, and reliability by their mothers thrive. Conversely, children who have been abused, criticized, or shunned by their mothers often suffer from low self-esteem, fears, awkwardness, detached personalities, and in severe cases, mental illnesses.

When we become joined to a new person spiritually and physically through marriage, we have the opportunity to form a new attachment foundation. Just as you were born of your mother's flesh, you are now one flesh with your mate. An exciting opportunity emerges for you to reprogram each other. In this divine union, your mate has the right and the ability to reprogram your self-image.

This is a sacred responsibility. Eventually the reprogramming happens, intentional or not. Therefore, couples must be aware of their power to transform the other. We can use this position to build up and edify the other, or we can misuse it to tear down and belittle.

Scripture admonishes us to love and respect each other as we do our own bodies. Become aware of your ability to reprogram your mate and strive to make this reprogramming a wonderful thing!

Ask the Lord for enlightenment in the areas where your spouse needs to be positively reprogrammed. Pray that the Lord will empower you to build up your mate with prayer and praise.

For this reason, a man shall leave his father and mother and shall be joined to his wife, and the two shall become one flesh. This mystery is great; but I am speaking with reference to Christ and the church. Nevertheless, each individual among you also is to love his own wife even as himself, and the wife must see to it that she respects her husband. **Ephesians 5:31-33**

A ten-year-old boy named Randy was asked jokingly how he would make a marriage work. "That's easy," said the boy. "You just keep telling your wife she's real purty [sic] even if other people think she looks like a truck!"

Well, maybe Randy has some insight into the reprogramming component of becoming one flesh. Your life has been a compilation of verdicts about yourself from mothers, fathers, siblings, teachers, friends, employers, pastors, etc. But when you get married, your partner has the power to overturn those verdicts in a single word. Have you noticed that? It does not matter what anyone else has said. If your partner says you are smart, capable, and attractive, you begin to believe it! Likewise, if your partner continues to demean and tear you down, all of the life-affirming work your parents may have done begins to crumble in an avalanche of crushed self-esteem.

When we get married, we entrust ourselves into someone else's hands. The groom places himself into his bride's hands, and the bride places herself into her groom's hands. Look down at your hand. Your wedding ring is a symbol of that trust. Never use your hands to crush a spirit. From this day forward, strive to make sure your hands are nurturing the one whose life you hold.

Start today. Tell your mate they are "real purty" even if he or she does look like a truck!

Pray for a kind and nurturing spirit toward the one whose wedding ring you wear.

Let no unwholesome word proceed from your mouth, but only such a word as is good for edification according to the need of the moment, so that it will give grace to those who hear. **Ephesians 4:29**

During the 70s, women began a new trend of short hair. In rebellion to the stiff hairdos and countless hours at the beauty parlors, women began to pursue a more maintenance free approach. We had a friend who decided to do something radical: she cut off all of her hair. She left her house with hair piled high in one of those up-dos that were popular then. Hair spray and pins, and things I know nothing about must have held her hairdo together. However, when she returned home, all of that was gone. Her hair was shorter than her husband's.

We were visiting their home that day. As she entered the living room, we all looked up, barely recognizing her. I have to admit, I was taken aback. Tears filled her eyes as she waited for reactions. Her husband slowly rose and walked toward her. Beaming, he said, "Now that's more like it! Now there is nothing to hide your beautiful face." Her tears turned to giggles as they embraced, and I saw her confidence return. She bustled around and began to be the confident, charming hostess she had always been - laughing, chatting, and making us all feel welcome.

Reprogramming. That husband really got it.

Pray for the ability to reprogram your spouse in a way that builds up, not tears down. Ask the Lord for fresh ways to edify your mate daily.

So husbands ought also to love their own wives as their own bodies. He who loves his own wife loves himself; for no one ever hated his own flesh, but nourishes and cherishes it, just as Christ also does the church, because we are members of His body.
Ephesians 5:28-30

A deep oneness can be born from reprogramming. If you establish an affirming environment in your home, your spouse will open up more and more, and deep intimacy will develop. Within the context of this safe environment, you will achieve the ability to talk about one another's faults. No one is perfect. Ignoring or glazing over flaws is not healthy. Careful and gentle reprogramming can help us recognize and improve on our shortcomings.

If your mate struggles with an imperfection, as we all do, be prayerful and careful about how you approach it. As the two of you reprogram and retool together, a bonding will take place that is indescribable. I am reminded of the loyalty and camaraderie military troops have for each other. Having been retooled by the assaults of battle, they emerge proud, loyal, and faithful to each other and to their cause.

Pray for the ability to create a home and a marriage that is a safe environment for openness and vulnerability.

So husbands ought also to love their own wives as their own bodies. He who loves his own wife loves himself; for no one ever hated his own flesh, but nourishes and cherishes it, just as Christ also does the church, because we are members of His body.
Ephesians 5:28-30

Edification is a powerful tool in marriage. As we have seen, we can reprogram in a negative way, or in a positive way. Edification builds up, increases confidence, and acts as a repellant to low self-esteem.

I saw a lovely Christian couple on a talk show. The young woman had been viciously attacked by a mountain lion while riding her bike through a national park. She recalled the moment when she said to herself, "He just tore my face off." And he had. The husband recalled rushing to the hospital and seeing his bride lying on the gurney, mangled and torn, fighting for her life. He answered the interviewer's questions:

"What did you think the first time you saw her?"
"I thanked God she was alive."
"We are looking at your honeymoon pictures on the split screen and can see what a beautiful woman she was."
"She still is."
"Well, yes, and a very lucky one," the anchor continued. "How did you feel when you looked in the mirror?" the interviewer asked the woman.

"Truthfully, I was horrified. For weeks I was completely bandaged. Then when they removed the bandages, I couldn't look. My husband would tell me daily that I was his beautiful wife. He would pray and read Scripture to me. As the days and weeks went by, I began to believe him. Finally I had the courage to look. It was shocking. I felt shame, but my husband would not hear of it. He kept telling me that he married me, not my face."

Her husband joined in: "We are Christians, and we believe it is the inside that matters. Through Christ, we are made new, clean, and beautiful. She is not the woman I married…she is stronger and she is better."

"Wow," stammered the news anchor. "What a story. Thanks to you both."

Reprogramming can help your spouse heal from many types of scars.

Ask the Lord to give you an unswerving desire to build openness and trust through the edification of each other.

So husbands ought also to love their own wives as their own bodies. He who loves his own wife loves himself; for no one ever hated his own flesh, but nourishes and cherishes it, just as Christ also does the church, because we are members of His body.

Ephesians 5:28-30

We have been looking at the three things that must be in place for you and your partner to become one flesh: joining, reprogramming, and performance. Today we will look at the third action, performance. How do you perform as a team? Are you on the same page when it comes to the big issues in life?

As we have seen, the head of the wife is the husband. Paul uses this image when he describes marriage. Therefore, the wife represents the body. So in performance, if the body turns right, but the head turns left, you have a problem. You must act in sync with each other.

Often I see couples that have found synchronicity in their sexual intimacy, but after they were married, things started to fall apart because they disagreed about parenting, about finances, and they disagreed about church.

The issue is simple. They have become partners and come together at times for sexual intimacy, but on all other accounts, they have remained separate entities. There has been no reprogramming to build each other up; there has been no joining or vulnerability, other than during sexual coupling; and often times, they have not co-mingled their finances. Basically, they are like two countries that come together occasionally for a big summit and then return to their own sovereign nation.

Oneness is established through participating in life as a team. As members of the same body, we are to nourish and cherish each part. If you have not joined together and reprogrammed each other, you will not be able to perform well together. Sexual intimacy will wane if it is the only performance you work on.

Pray for a keen awareness of each other's needs and desires. Ask God to help you perform as a team in all areas of your marriage.

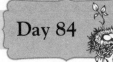

Do you not know that your bodies are members of Christ? Shall I then take away the members of Christ and make them members of a prostitute? May it never be! Or do you not know that the one who joins himself to a prostitute is one body with her? For He says, "THE TWO SHALL BECOME ONE FLESH." But the one who joins himself to the Lord is one spirit with Him. Flee immorality. Every other sin that a man commits is outside the body, but the immoral man sins against his own body. Or do you not know that your body is a temple of the Holy Spirit who is in you, whom you have from God, and that you are not your own? For you have been bought with a price: therefore glorify God in your body. **I Corinthians 6:15-20**

Physical oneness should come as a celebration of spiritual oneness. After we have been spiritually united through covenant, joining, and reprogramming, we have the great reward of being sexually intimate with our partner. The truth is, you cannot separate the spiritual from the physical. The spirit is as much a part of the human being as is the body.

When the Corinthian church was satisfying their sexual drives by engaging in relations with prostitutes, the Spirit of God led Paul to admonish them to stop. The reasoning he presented gives us interesting insight into something that happens when two people come together sexually. When they join physically, they also join spiritually. Paul tells the Corinthians they should not have sex with prostitutes because they become one with the prostitute. That fits everything we have learned about becoming one flesh. He says when Christians have intercourse with a prostitute, they are bringing Christ, who lives in them, into union with a prostitute.

1. If you are a Christian, your body is a member of Christ. (v. 15)

2. Having sex with a prostitute makes the Christian one body with the prostitute. (v.16)

3. The applied argument is that Christians having sex with a prostitute somehow sets up a situation where Christ is one with her, and Jesus did not intend to be part of that. (vv. 19-20)

Do you see how it works? When we become one with Christ and we have sex outside of marriage, that oneness is taking place with Jesus Christ. The Christian is having more than a physical union with her. He is also having a spiritual union with her that neither Jesus nor the Holy Spirit can have any part of. This leads us to believe that when married couples join together in the marriage bed, they join more than their bodies. They join their spirits. Are you joining your spirit with a mate who is joined with Christ?

Pray that your marriage bed would bring the joy and pleasure that comes with spiritual unity in Christ Jesus.

The man said, "This is now bone of my bones, and flesh of my flesh; she shall be called woman, because she was taken out of man." **Genesis 2:23**

Today we continue our look at marital chemistry and physical oneness to see how they develop along temperamental lines and gender lines. Temperament is the way we deal with the world. People look at the world through different eyes. Some people believe the world is a wonderful, friendly place, while others believe the world is dangerous and unfriendly. Some are proactive and get going before someone else beats them to it. Still others are laid-back, and sit and wait for things to happen, and then react. Put all this together, and you have different kinds of temperaments.

So, when we become one flesh with our marriage partner, two different temperaments must now coexist. We are suddenly forced to see the world through someone else's temperament. In the chemistry department, this can shake things up. Are you a proactive lover, or a laid back one? Do you expect good things for and from your mate, or are you the type who expects bad from the world? There is a danger that the two temperaments can deride the physical intimacy in a marriage.

However, there is a much greater opportunity for it to enrich your love-life! From the position of one flesh, I am now able to see life as Jo Beth sees it. She is a calmer and more methodical person by nature than I am. On the other hand, Jo Beth is able to embrace the excitement and energy with which I view the world. As we have become one, our different temperaments have enhanced and enriched our connection.

Gender lines likewise play into marital chemistry. One of the best parts of being married is having a complete view of the world – both from the feminine perspective and the masculine perspective. As I have lived with and loved my wife, I have a richer outlook than I did when I lived life from an all-male perspective. I can see things through her lens, and she can see through mine.

Embrace each other…in every way!

Pray for enhanced and enriched chemistry as you embrace each other's temperaments, becoming one flesh with two temperaments.

Then the LORD God said, "It is not good for the man to be alone; I will make him a helper suitable for him." **Genesis 2:18**

Cardinal Point East on the Happy Home compass is friendship, or companionship. In the beginning, God said, "It is not good for man to be alone." Herein, we find the purpose of marriage: companionship.

I read a story about an elderly couple who had been married 72 years. As best friends in their teens, they had become engaged and married to each other within twelve hours. On May 26, 1939, she graduated high school at 10:00 am, and they were married at 10:00 pm that same evening.

"They just genuinely liked each other," the son told the interviewer. "They always worked as a team. Everything was done together as a rule. We rarely saw them apart."

They traveled together, worked at a car dealership together, and played sports together. So it came as no surprise that they were together when a car accident sent them to the hospital – both having sustained serious injuries. People say that each was asking about the other. Her back was badly damaged, but she kept asking about her husband. Through his pain, he relentlessly asked the nurses to check on his wife.

When it became obvious that the injuries were life threatening, they were placed in a room together side by side. They immediately joined hands. He was the first to pass away. But something strange happened. His heart monitor kept going. Hopeful, one of their children asked the nurse, "Look, are you sure he is gone? Why is his heart beating?"

Gently, the nurse replied, "They are holding hands so tightly; your mother's heart is beating through him."

And so it always had been. She joined him one hour later. His son closed the story with this, "Dad always said a good woman was worth waiting for. I believe he went on ahead, and waited an hour for her to join him to meet the Lord together."

It is not good for man to be alone.

Pray that you will establish an enduring friendship with your mate.

Then the LORD God said, "It is not good for the man to be alone; I will make him a helper suitable for him." **Genesis 2:18**

A nother word about Cardinal Point East on the Happy Home compass: Friendship and companionship are life-enhancing blessings. We have seen that God said, "It is not good for man to be alone." However, in the garden, Adam was already satisfied with life because he had an intimate, unadulterated relationship with his Creator. Therefore, Eve, his wife, was another vehicle through which God showed His love to Adam.

A very real danger exists of making an idol out of marriage. Marriage is the manifestation of Christ's love for us. As we have seen in Ephesians, the husband is compared to the head – which is Christ – and the wife is compared to the body – which is the Church. In this there is a sacred balance.

The companionship of a lover is a physical manifestation of God's love and friendship with us. However, we must never place too big of a burden on our mate's shoulders to fulfill us. Only Christ can fill our emptiness. Our mate is merely a friend and a companion to come alongside us, to recognize that emptiness and point us toward Christ.

We have to understand that the real Bridegroom is Christ. Without this foundational direction, you will always be demanding more of your spouse than he or she can possibly deliver.

Give thanks to the Lord today for the wonderful blessing of marriage. Thank Him for giving you a glimpse into how much He loves you through the friendship of marriage.

A friend loves at all times, and a brother is born for adversity. **Proverbs 17:17**

C.S. Lewis said of friendship: "It is when we are doing things together that friendship springs up – painting, sailing ships, praying, philosophizing, and fighting shoulder to shoulder. Friends look in the same direction."

Are you looking in the same direction as your mate? So often we become preoccupied with the business and the demands of life, and we forget to nurture our friendship with our bride or groom. This is especially true in the family with young children. A Happy Home is often a chaotic home. We tend to gear up for chores with a "divide and conquer" mentality.

This can be a dangerously slippery slope. Teamwork is foundational to friendship. Work together to get the children bathed, supper cooked, and dishes put away. If there is no time left at the end of the day for recreation and fellowship with your mate, leave something undone. Dirty dishes never lead to divorce. Lack of a friend and a companion can.

Be creative in your friendship. Not every couple can paint and sail, as C.S. Lewis suggests. But every couple can and should pray together and fight shoulder to shoulder. Use your resources to carve out a way to enter into friendship every day, and then when there is time, you can enjoy the smooth sailing.

Ask the Lord to inspire creativity in your quest for times of friendship and fun.

Put on then, as God's chosen ones, holy and beloved, compassionate hearts, kindness, humility, meekness, and patience, bearing with one another and, if one has a complaint against another, forgiving each other; as the Lord has forgiven you, so you also must forgive. And above all these put on love, which binds everything together in perfect harmony. **Colossians 3:12-14**

A Happy Home has friendship as its signature characteristic. First and foremost, the husband and wife must be friends. Within this environment of friendship and companionship, children become more secure and comfortable. They actually like being at home. Friends will flock to a home where the husband and wife enjoy and support each other.

One of my sons had a friend who seemed to never go home. When I would poke my head in to see my three sons sleeping, I could almost always count on a fourth head. When I asked my son why his friend never went home, he shrugged and said, "I guess we are just always having so much fun here, Dad."

A Happy Home is full of friendship and full of fun.

Prayerfully evaluate the level of friendship in your home. Ask the Lord to spring up a fresh measure of fun and fellowship.

"For I know the plans that I have for you," declares the Lord, "Plans for welfare and not for calamity; to give you a future and a hope." **Jeremiah 29:11**

> *Grow old along with me!*
> *The best is yet to be,*
> *The last of life, for which the first was made:*
> *Our times are in His hand.*
> *Who saith "A whole I planned,*
> *Youth shows but half; trust God: see all, nor be afraid!"*

Poet Robert Browning penned these words. They are very special to me because they were the words that Jo Beth's uncle read as he married us. When I read those words, the years roll back as if it was yesterday, and I am transported back to that day so long ago in Mississippi. I can see my bride and me standing at the altar. The thrill, the nerves, the hope, and the weight of the moment all come rushing back to me. I believe each young couple shares the hope that we had standing there on the brink of our future, that Robert Browning's words would be true, "the best is yet to be."

For us, I can honestly say the words rang resoundingly true. Our marriage and our home have not been perfect; we are imperfect people, but we do have a perfect Savior Who has blessed, redeemed, healed, forgiven, and thrilled us! Each day dawns with hope. I have been blessed to go through life with my best friend at my side.

As we end this ninety-day journey together, I want to encourage you to be intentional about establishing your Happy Home. I know with the Lord Jesus Christ as your building foundation, the best is yet to be!

Pray for application of God's truths for a Happy Home. Ask Him to encourage you that He has a plan and a future for your family.

About the Author

Dr. H. Edwin Young is the author of *Healing Broken America, Light Walking,* and *The Ten Commandments of Marriage*. He is the senior pastor of one of America's largest churches, Second Baptist Church of Houston. During his three decades as pastor, Second has experienced tremendous growth, with a current membership exceeding 60,000. Under his leadership, the church has pioneered the concept of "one church in multiple locations" and currently has five campuses in the greater Houston community. He and his wife, Jo Beth have three grown sons and ten grandchildren.

If you are ever in the Houston area please join us for worship at Second. For service times and locations go to second.org.

Second Baptist Church
6400 Woodway
Houston, Texas 77057

Dr. Young can be seen and heard throughout the world via the radio, television, and Internet ministry of the *Winning Walk*. In the U.S., the broadcast goes out to over 50 million households; internationally, *Winning Walk* is broadcast on six continents. For a broadcast schedule or to learn more, visit us at *winningwalk.org*.

Other Books by Ed Young

Healing Broken America
Light Walking
Living Under the Rainbow
Standing on the Promises
Total Heart Health for Women
Total Heart Health for Men
The 10 Commandments of Parenting
The 10 Commandments of Marriage
Everlasting Father
Everywhere I Go
Pure Sex
Expressions of Love
Been There, Done That, Now What?
Romancing the Home
Against All Odds
The Winning Walk
The Purpose of Suffering
David, After God's Own Heart
The Lord Is…